Scribble Art

Independent Creative
Art Experiences for Children

MaryAnn F. Kohl

illustrations
Judy McCoy

BRIGHT IDEAS
FOR LEARNING

Bright Ring
Publishing

CREDITS

Illustrations   **Judy McCoy**
Typography   **textype**
Cover Design **MaryAnn and Mike Kohl**
Photography   **Tore Ofteness**

ISBN 0-935607-05-6

Library of Congress Catalog Card Number 94-94502

COPYRIGHT © 1994 MaryAnn F. Kohl

Manufactured in the United States of America   1st printing 1994
10   9   8   7   6   5   4

ATTENTION: SCHOOLS AND BUSINESSES

Publisher's Cataloging in Publication

(Prepared by Quality Books Inc.)

Kohl, MaryAnn F.
     Scribble art : independent creative art experiences for children
/ author, MaryAnn F. Kohl; illustrator, Judy McCoy. -- 2nd ed.
     p. cm. -- (Bright ideas for learning ; 4)
     Rev. ed. of: Scribble cookies. c1985.
     Includes index.
     Preassigned LCCN: 94-94502.
     ISBN 0-935607-05-6

     1. Handicraft--Juvenile Literature. I. McCoy, Judy. II. Kohl, Mary Ann. Scribble cookies. III. Title. IV. Series: Kohl, MaryAnn F. Bright ideas for learning; 4.

TT160.K65 1994   745.5
                                          QBI94-1270

DEDICATION

To my husband, Michael, and my daughters, Hannah and Megan.

michael   Hannah   megan   mary ann

ACKNOWLEDGEMENTS

Thank you, former students from Mountain View Elementary School, Ferndale, Washington, for your creativity and your beautiful inner spirits. With you I learned as I taught, and with you I found creativity came from within you, not from my teaching you how.

Sterling Brand, principal of Mountain View Elementary School, encouraged creativity and individuality in the teachers who worked with him, thereby encouraging us to do the same with our students.

Marlene McCracken, author and master teacher, taught me the philosophy that children learn by doing, that teachers find success by guiding children in their individuality, and that all children can achieve if given the time and respect to do so.

Special thanks to: textype, Trish Lemon and Dorothy Tjoelker-Worthen; BookCrafters, Donna Shankleton; WestPro Graphics, Arthur Mole; and Tore Ofteness, Photography.

Sofie   Basil   Clara

"Every time we teach a child something, we keep him from inventing it himself. On the other hand, that which we allow him to discover for himself, will remain with him visible...for the rest of his life."

– John Piaget

LETTER TO THE ARTIST

Dear Artist:

Are you ready to enter the world of creativity, where there is no right or wrong way to create? Imagine feeling free to encounter any art experience without a set of rules or expectations for outcomes!

I like to say, "Process not Product," which means: the doing, exploring, creating, and attempting of new ideas is more important than the result of your creativity. You may end up with a painting resembling a muddy smear, but if you tried something new, learned something interesting, or discovered how paint acts, then you had a successful art process. The product is not as important.

However, if you would still like a nice art product, all the art ideas in this book are easy, creative, and interesting, and can turn out to be quite amazing and fun.

The art experiences found in this book were tested by children and then compiled for the purpose of independent art expression and experiences for artists of all ages. These art techniques and ideas are the same as those used by professional artists, but you can explore art and its process, rather than working towards the end product of art as a goal. When you are ready and have explored the process of art, go ahead and try for a finished product you would enjoy. Anything goes!

Think of your art as "experiments". Some things will look great and others won't, but what you learn and discover in the process is worth so much more than perfect looking results. Go ahead and recycle or reuse your experiments or save your favorite artworks. Think of ways to use your experiments for other art ideas, too. There is no right or wrong way to create with the ideas in this book.

Each art experience can be set up in an independent art center at home or at school and enjoyed and explored without adult samples to copy. Gather some materials and supplies from the kitchen or classroom and then, with a general technique with which to get started, you create, explore, discover, and express.

There is no right or wrong way for the art ideas in this book to turn out. There is only your way, the way of the artist. You, the artist, need only please yourself.

I hope you will enjoy creating and discovering as you drip, smudge, glop, and sculpt your way through this book over the next few hours, weeks, years, or a lifetime! Oh, I almost forgot. Don't forget to help clean up!

Write soon!

Your friend,

MaryAnn Kohl

MaryAnn F. Kohl
author

THE INDEPENDENT ART CENTER

How to set up an art center: Encourage Independence

Select a corner of the room or a table that will be the center of art activities. This area will be "child ready" with supplies at child level: scissors in a can, pencils, brushes, crayons, glue, tape, stapler, and other commonly used materials. Keep a supply of paper, newspaper, paper towels, collage items, sewing trims, ink pad, empty cups, and other items often used for art on hand. Always keep a scrap box filled and ready to go.

Have a shelf or cupboard nearby at child level to hold materials. Use shoe boxes, plastic trays, coffee cans, or other inexpensive containers to organize materials. In all cases, remember that the art center will be dripped and splattered, so use materials than can be cleaned or materials that can be enjoyed without concern for ultimate cleanliness.

Many activities will only need a refreshing of materials that are always on hand, needing little or no adult direction. Other activities will require some explanation for simple art techniques or safety. Children should, however, be supervised at all times.

Most important, under no circumstances should an adult make a sample for the artist to copy. The art in this book is open-ended, and is provided to encourage each child to experience the process of creative art rather than a finished product. The finished product is an outcome of exploration and creativity, not the goal. Therefore, no finished product samples are necessary.

Special art materials will be provided periodically in the center. Simple explanations of how to get started are often the only "teaching" necessary for these activities. Let creativity takes it course. You will be pleasantly surprised and often amazed at the outcomes of creative exploration by children of all ages.

The adult in charge should keep an eye on the art center and assist in keeping it tidy and child ready. Of course, children should be responsible for cleaning up after themselves; thus, keep a trash bin and recycling containers handy, provide a dust broom and pan, a sink or bucket of soapy water, a sponge, and other cleaning materials.

Encourage independence, encourage creativity, and encourage fun. And prepare to see amazing art process from the natural imaginations of children.

Why a center? "The art center is a safe place to create."

A center takes the pressure off a child to copy or compete with other children for style, speed, and quantity. A child should be able to work at the art center for as long as he needs, to create as many or as few expressions and explorations as he needs, and to create in his own way without an adult-made sample to copy. The art center feels like·a safe place to create and explore possibilities. The art center is therefore a creative place to explore and discover.

The art center benefits the adult as well as the child. It takes very little preparation or planning to keep an art center supplied as compared to setting up and preparing specific art materials for a unique art project each day. Once a center is established, materials only need be added or changed when the supplies run low or a new idea pops into the picture. New ideas and supplies then become a part of the art center's regular supply; safety and basic techniques have been introduced, and the artist can then be independent and feel comfortable exploring and creating.

Providing a new set of materials with no direction is an exciting experience for the artist and the adult. Children will use the materials as you might expect, and also, in entirely new and expressive ways. All artistic endeavor is unique and has merit.

The artist should be able to move freely from the art center to other centers or activities upon completion of his art exploration. Simple rules such as cleaning up before leaving the center help keep things running smoothly. Help the artist out by setting up an area for drying projects, a cubby for work to take home or save, and a system of choosing other activities upon completion.

Above all, each child should be encouraged to be independent in artistic process rather than striving for a finished product. Independence and responsibility in choosing materials, techniques, and then in cleaning up and moving on to something else are skills that learned early will benefit the child as he grows to adulthood.

Watching children explore, discover, create, and succeed in the process of art is a wonderful experience for the adult. I always tell children, "There is no right way or wrong way for your art idea to turn out...there is only your way." I've seen eyes light up time and time again as young artists realize that creativity is not a rigid science but rather is a process with no one to judge the experience but themselves. Remember, Process Not Product!

GUIDELINES

THE ICONS

Positioned in the upper right corner of each art experience page are icons which help the parent, teacher, or artist evaluate that particular project as to the following:

EXPERIENCE LEVEL: The experience icon is positioned at the corner of each art project to assist in choosing, not to limit children from choosing. To help make the selection of art projects more precise and to help match skill levels of children, the projects are labeled with icons of:

* one star for beginning artists with little experience (easy)
** two stars for artists with some art experience (intermediate or moderate)
*** three stars for the more experienced artist (advanced or complicated)

Age and skill do not necessarily go hand and hand. Therefore, the experience icon flags which projects are for new or beginning-level artists, mid-level artists with some experience, and advanced-level artists with greater experience. However, all children can explore all projects whether the skill level matches their own or not. They may just need a little extra help.

 BASIC ART: Some art experiences are fundamental or basic to all other projects. For instance, Fingerpainting is fundamental to Fingerpaint Mono-print. Doing a basic fingerpainting before the mono-print will give more success, understanding, and experience to the mono-print. Art ideas that are basic should be experienced by all children for a well balanced art program and are marked with an apple for "Basic" or fundamental. These art experiences should not be missed and can be repeated over and over.

ART TECHNIQUE: The art icon shows which art medium is used in the project.

painting/   drawing/   chalk   sculpture   dough/   collage/   printing
dye   coloring   mixture   construction/
                                              craft

PLANNING/PREPARATION: The planning and preparation icon indicates the degree of involvement and time for the adult in charge.

*Note: Shown in Chart of Contents as:
◆ easy ◆◆ moderate ◆◆◆ involved

easy   moderate   involved

 CAUTION: When electrical, sharp, hot, or adult tools are used in a project, the caution sign indicates that extra care and close supervision is necessary for the child. An adult should do the more hazardous or difficult steps or assist the artist carefully.

 HELP: Sometimes a project is not necessarily dangerous, but some assistance may be needed from another child or another person.

 AUTHOR'S FAVORITE: The author has chosen several favorite projects in each chapter which are indicated with a heart with the author's initials inside it. These are the projects that MaryAnn Kohl has found to be not only her favorites, but the favorites of many children as well.

 OVERVIEW: Each project and its process is summarized and evaluated at the top of each page. Read these as an aid in deciding if a project is appropriate or appealing.

BASIC ART MATERIALS

The following list of art supplies provide a wonderful well-rounded selection for any art program for kids of all ages. Collect and purchase what you can. Remember, buying in bulk can save money and that saving free materials can build a rich supply of art materials. *Those materials with stars are of absolute necessity if children are to begin the most basic of art experiences.*

*art tissue: Tissue paper in many colors of the rainbow. Can be purchased in packs of one color, or a mixture of colors. Use for many art ideas such as those in the Materials Index listed under art tissue.

brayer: A roller especially designed for making prints. A rolling pin can be used in place of a brayer.

butcher paper: Heavy gauge paper on wide rolls in many colors from school supply stores. Also available in the grocery store as white paper on a roll, but not much wider than wax paper. Great for many art projects. Check the Materials Index for suggestions.

cardboard: Many uses. Primarily for sculpture or as the base for other projects.

coffee filters: Useful for art ideas involving dying with food coloring, powdered vegetable dye, or watercolor paint.

*collage items: See the list of collage items at the end of this book for detailed, alphabetical suggestions. Items to save for collage range from paper scraps to jewelry.

colored chalk: Look for soft, bright chalk that is not scratchy or labeled "for chalkboards only". Sometimes called pastels.

contact paper, clear: Clear plastic with pull-away backing. Contact paper sticks to almost all surfaces. Use to cover paper to save designs or as the art surface.

*crayons: Crayola is still the best, but any crayons will do. Keep stubs, peel them, and use for additional crayon projects.

darning needle, plastic: Young children use for sewing and stitching with yarn on cardboard, styrofoam trays, or other materials and fabrics. Has large eye and not as sharp as regular needles.

embroidery floss: Useful for all projects that ask for yarn or thread. Rainbow of colors. Expensive but scraps can be gathered from many people for a nice selection.

*fabric scraps: Save all types of fabric scraps for art such as gluing to paper or cardboard, sewing, weaving, or other decorating uses.

*felt pens (marking pens): Come in many styles and qualities, from fine tip to broad, from water based to permanent. Good pens last the longest. Permanent markers should be supervised because they really are permanent!

*flour, salt, cornstarch, baking soda: Useful for many dough and playdough recipes as well as homemade paste, paint, and other glazes. See the recipe section of this book for suggestions.

*food coloring, liquid: Substitute in most projects that require paint or dye. Good for paper dying, coloring dough, and for printing projects.

food coloring, paste: Use in same projects as liquid food coloring, but is more concentrated and goes farther than liquid. Use in art calling for powdered vegetable dye.

framing scraps: Framing shops have a multitude of wooden framing scraps available for free. Provide the framer with a box and the framer will fill it with scraps with characteristics such as gold, fabric, carvings, and wonderful designs.

*glitter: Place in a salt or cheese shaker. Excess glitter can be slipped back into the shaker or a new container for mixed colors of glitter by lifting the edges of the news-paper and letting the glitter fall into the fold of the paper.

glue, tacky (hobby): Tacky glue is thicker and stickier than white glue. Especially useful for fabric gluing.

*glue, white: Usually known as Elmer's Glue or, in Canada, Le Page's Glue. A basic to hundreds of art ideas. Can be thinned with water and used as a glaze or used as is for gluing paper and other materials.

glue gun: To be used only with adult supervision or by the adult for quick, solid gluing. Never leave a child unattended with a glue gun.

hole punch (paper punch): Useful for punching holes in cardboard, paper, tag board, and other materials. The holes from the punch are also useful as confetti and other decoration. Invest in a heavy duty punch for punching holes in thick paper, several layers of paper, or posterboard.

ink pad: For printing with rubber stamps or self-designed stamps made of other materials. Come in many colors. Refill bottles can be purchased to re-ink a dry pad.

iron (old): An old iron comes in handy for many art projects such as melting crayon between wax paper pieces or in transferring fabric crayon designs from paper to fabric. Also good for flattening curled paintings.

*masking tape: Sturdy brown tape in several different widths which tears or cuts. Can be peeled off again from most surfaces if not left on too long.

*matte board: A basic supply for art, matte board can be collected for free in all shapes, colors, and sizes from framing shops. Provide the shop with a box and pick up a full box of matte board every couple of weeks or so.

*newsprint: Available from local printers, printers' supply stores, and from newspaper printers. Also available from moving and shipping companies. Use newspaper or newsprint interchangably. Newspaper has the print and newsprint is plain and clean.

oil pastels: A combination of chalk and crayon available from art or hobby stores. Brighter and less smudgy than chalk, but blends better than crayon.

*paintbrushes: Brushes come in many shapes and sizes. For quality results, buy quality brushes. Most school supply stores carry some nice ones for easel painting and watercolor.

*paper: All kinds, all colors, from stores or saved from the recycle bin at a print shop. Save a variety. Cut into shapes or smaller pieces. Use both sides to extend use.

paper scraps: All papers, from junk to art paper, eventually become scraps. Save for all kinds of art projects.

*paste: Paste comes in jars with brushes, is non-toxic, and works in ways glue can't. Can be mixed with paint for color.

pastels: Soft art chalk in many colors. Usually has squared edges rather than round.

pencils: Pencils come in handy when lines need to be erased, for general drawing, for tracing, and for delicate rubbings. Colored pencils are good for older children or for young children who have some experience in drawing with crayon and regular pencils.

play clay: Sometimes called Plasticine. A commercial product in bright colors. Will not harden or dry out. Can stain. Useful for many art experiences. See Materials Index.

*scissors: Don't skimp on the quality of scissors. Good sharp scissors are a basic for children and are available with blunt ends for safety.

*stapler: Little hands can work medium to large staplers quite well. Avoid the tiny staplers. Show kids how to fill a stapler and have one less job to worry about.

*starch, liquid: Use to mix paint to a smooth consistency for a glaze over paper projects, or as a glue substitute. Available in the laundry section of grocery stores and in the art section of school supply stores.

*styrofoam grocery tray: Useful as the base of many art projects, as a container for paint or glue, to sort or store collage items, and to cut up for other art uses. Wash and dry before using. Some stores will donate trays or sell them for a fair price.

tape (all kinds): Keep a supply of tape - cellophane, duct, masking, library - any kinds at all. Kids never seem to have enough tape suitable for all jobs. Note the new masking tapes in pretty colors.

tempera paint, liquid: Liquid tempera paint is usually thick enough that it still needs to be thinned with water and liquid starch for painting. Liquid tempera is more expensive than powdered but offers some convenience in that it is already mixed and generally usable.

*tempera paint, powdered: Dry tempera paint has many uses and art techniques and comes in many colors. If you don't have much money, buy the basic primary colors of paint and mix all other colors you would like from red, yellow, and blue. Buy white, too, to make pastel colors, but you can do without black if you're saving money.

vegetable dye, powdered: Available in bulk from school supply stores. Useful as a transparent paint when mixed as found in the recipe section of this book. Has many other art uses such as paper dying and batik. Use in any project calling for food coloring, and many projects calling for tempera paint.

watercolor paint: Comes in tubes, blocks, or paintboxes. Paintboxes and blocks work best for children. Use a good brush and good paper for best results.

wood scraps: Save pieces from a frame shop, shop class, or construction site for sculptures or for the base of other art work. Can be painted, glued, nailed, or used as a printing tool.

*yarn: Save scraps of all colors, all textures, and all styles. Keep yarn rolled in balls and stick the loose end through a hole in a box for a yarn dispenser. Useful for art, for weaving, hanging, or sewing.

Chart of Contents

PAPER AND COLLAGE
chapter 1

CUT-AND-PASTE

 Cutting and pasting paper is one of the most satisfying art experiences for artists of any age because of the open ended possibilities and the room for imagination and inventiveness. There are no bounds to the types of papers available either. Make friends with a print shop and have them save scraps in a box for the artists.

MATERIALS

any of the following papers or scraps –

greeting cards	wallpaper	facial tissue	junk mail
wrapping paper	bags and sacks	typing paper	brochures
scraps	newspaper	rice paper	posters
magazines	catalogs	onion skin paper	photos
food wrappers	art tissue	tracing paper	cardboard
file folders	matte board	paper towels	napkins
envelopes	tag board	printer's scraps	drawings

things to stick and bind with –

glue	paste	glue sticks	tape
stapler	scissors	stickers	hole punch
masking tape	duct tape	needle/thread	string
ribbons	yarn	sewing scraps	brads
paper clips	labels	contact paper	labels

other things to encourage cut and paste creativity –

crayons	paints	felt pens	pencils
chalk	scribble cookies	layered muffins	charcoal

PROCESS

1. Provide any paper on hand and items to use for sticking and binding. Allow for complete freedom and exploration.
2. Cut and paste or stick paper to other papers. Dry.

VARIATIONS

- Suggest themes for cut-and-paste such as –

emotions	nutrition	family	litter
holidays	alphabet	gifts	love
counting	seasons	children	happiness
wishes	travel	pets	cultures

- Pre-cut pictures from magazines and have them in a box ready to use, such as pictures about –

good food	friends	family	pets
favorites	emotions	colors	so on

TORN PAPER DESIGN

MATERIALS
scraps of construction paper
other paper scraps
sheet of paper
glue

 Tearing paper is a skill that precedes using scissors. Most children prefer scissors to tearing even if they have the control to tear paper the way they want it to come out. Therefore, encourage the fun of tearing paper, the unique rough edges, and the unexpected results.

PROCESS
1. Tear pieces of construction paper or other paper into pieces to glue onto a larger piece of paper.
2. Arrange the torn pieces on the paper.
3. Glue the pieces to the paper in a random design or a more specific scene or picture.

HINTS
- Allow children to experiment with tearing before the idea of gluing a finished design is introduced.
- Designs may be random and unplanned or realistic and planned.

VARIATION
- Use discarded papers for torn design such as –

newspaper	greeting cards	drawings
gift wrap	coloring books	used homework
posters	photographs	junk mail

random

realistic

PAPER COLLAGE

For the youngest child to the oldest adult, paper collage is a universal art medium that never grows tiresome. The possibilities are always changing based on the materials at hand and the age and imagination of the artist. Collage can be flat or three dimensional, and paper is versatile in its creative possibilities.

MATERIALS

Collect a variety of papers and scraps such as –

wallpaper	posters	magazines
construction paper	tissue	printer's scraps
greeting cards	newspaper	napkins
wrapping paper	grocery bags	cupcake liners

glue or paste
scissors
a base for the collage, such as –

cardboard	paper	old file folder
matte board	box	box lid
styrofoam grocery tray		wood

PROCESS

1. Cut and glue paper in a random or planned approach on the selected base.
2. Cover the entire base, if desired, overlapping edges so the base does not show through.
3. Dry overnight.
4. When dry, coat the collage with white glue for a shiny clear cover.

VARIATIONS

- Create a theme paper collage such as –

happiness	Christmas	litter	pets
friends	family	wishes	dreams

All the pictures could relate to the theme of the collage.
- Work in a group and create a huge collage. Sneak in photographs of individual artists.
- Cover a Paper Collage with clear contact paper and use the collage for a placemat, an alphabet search, animal search, or other games using wash-off pens. Do not use glue.

3-D PAPER EXPERIMENTS

MATERIALS
scraps of construction paper
scraps of other papers
matte board or construction paper for the base
glue
tape
stapler
pencil
hole punch

From the simple to the complex, building and constructing with paper scraps has infinite possibilities. Some artists enjoy creating a "bug playground" or a "pixie village" with curly paper to climb and loops and shoots to play on. Others prefer to see just what they can make the paper do. Expect some giggling with this activity.

roll

PROCESS
1. Artists experiment with paper scraps and shapes to make them "stand up" from the base paper.
2. Artists may cut, tear, tape, staple, glue, or use scraps as they are. The possibilities are open.

Some art techniques for 3-D paper are –

bend	frill	punch	tear
bow	fringe	ridge	tie
braid	furrow	roll	tuck
crease	gather	score	tuft
crimp	knot	scrape	twist
curl	loop	slit	wad
curve	pleat	soften	warp
cut	plume	spiral	wrinkle
fold	pucker	tassel	weave

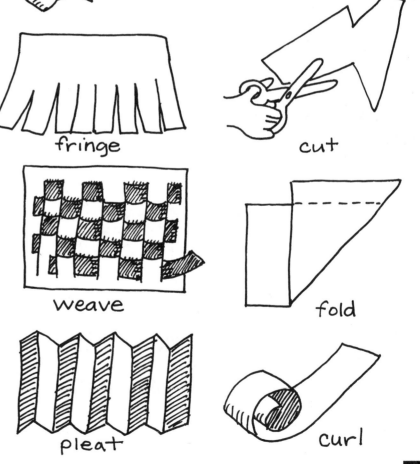

fringe

cut

weave

fold

pleat

curl

VARIATIONS
- Colors on a black background are effective. If several experiments are done on black backgrounds, they can all be joined into one display for a large group experiment.
- Provide many shapes, colors, and types of paper to motivate creativity.

Remember making snowflakes as children, with all the little cuts, holes, and little left-over scraps? Cut Paper Design builds on this concept but adds other dimensions to the snowflakes we knew so well. Think in terms of folding any shape of paper into any pattern, and then cut larger or more numerous holes leaving less paper than holes. Save the scraps, too, for other art ideas.

MATERIALS

thin paper, such as copier or typing bond
sheet of colored paper for base (optional)
scissors
glue

PROCESS

1. Fold the thin bond paper into a small square, triangle, or other shape.
2. Cut shapes, holes, slits, and designs from the paper until there is very little paper remaining. (Save the holes for other paper scrap projects.)
3. Next carefully unfold the cut paper design.
4. Glue the design down on a background of colored paper, if desired, or display in a window as is.

VARIATIONS

- Create snowflakes.
- Cut a shape such as a star, heart, flower, or apple. Then fold and cut the shape as described above.
- Mount the cut design on a background of wallpaper, gift wrap, poster, magazine picture, original drawing or colored art tissue. The colors and designs will show through the cuts and holes.
- For a multi-colored background, glue or tape small individual colored scraps over each hole on the back of the cut design.

SCORED PAPER

MATERIALS
typing paper or copier paper
cutting tools, such as –
    scissors in several sizes, ruler, X-acto knife
    (X-acto knife used only with adult supervision)
pencil
crayons or felt pens (optional)
tape (optional)
glue (optional)

PROCESS
1. Cut designs into paper with any of the cutting tools. Paper may be folded, punctured, or handled in any way the artist chooses. Some artists first draw lightly with a pencil to decide where to cut.
2. When cuts, slits, holes, or other designs have been cut, the cut paper can then be folded out or scored to stand away from the paper.
3. When a design is complete, the paper may be further decorated with crayons or colored pens, taped, stapled, or otherwise formed into a further sculpted shape, or left as it is with cut designs and no color.

VARIATIONS
- Stand the paper on edge and roll it to resemble a lantern.
  Tape the loose edges together. Set a votif candle in a protective glass container inside the lantern and see the lights shine through all the scored and cut designs. Be cautious and supervise candles at all times.
- Create a lantern or luminaria with a paper lunch sack.
  Be cautious and supervise candles at all times.

 Scored Paper is like a sculpture made by cutting little holes, slits, and cuts which can then be folded out or removed. The designs can range from a snowflake look to a complex architectural structure with spires and windows.

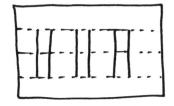 score and cut

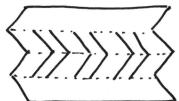 fold

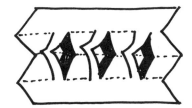 fold out cuts

 roll, tape and punch holes

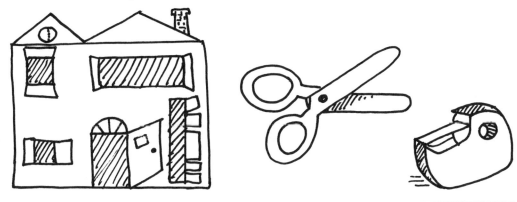

SPRINKLE DOTS

 What is it about sprinkling confetti on glue that makes everyone feel so good? This easy-to-do art experience requires little expertise or material, but is always a pleasure in the process of sprinkling and gluing. Make your own dots or purchase bags of commercial ones made from plastic, ribbons, or paper.

MATERIALS
confetti
tiny scraps
holes saved from paper punch
white glue thinned with water in a cup
paintbrush
sheet of paper for base
newspaper

PROCESS
1. Brush some thinned glue over part of the base paper.
2. Sprinkle or place confetti on the sticky areas.
3. Brush with more thinned glue.
4. Shake excess dots and confetti onto a piece of newspaper.
5. Proceed until the base paper is covered in a desired design.
6. Dry completely.

VARIATIONS
- This identical process can be followed with confetti and sprinkles on a block of wood, matte board, glass jar, wax paper, rock, or other base.
- Sprinkle Dots is an effective design worked over a crayon drawing, and can resemble snow, magic, outer space, night sky, or celebration.
- Follow this idea using any small sprinkly items such as –

sewing scraps	any paper punched with hole punch
sand	rice
art tissue bits	salt
rock salt	cut scraps from snowflakes

PAPER MOSAIC

MATERIALS
colored paper scraps or magazine pictures
scissors
egg carton
pencil
paste
hat pin or darning needle, optional
paper or matte board for base

 Patience is needed for placing tiny bits of paper on a precise design or drawing. But artists can also sprinkle bits of paper on glue lines for a freer, more casual approach to mosaics. For inspiration, look in a book at mosaics from Italy made with colored tiles.

PROCESS
1. Cut colored paper into small uniform sizes and sort into an egg carton by color.
2. Make a light pencil drawing on the base paper if desired.
3. Apply paste to individual pieces and place them on the drawing. A hat pin or needle will help in picking up the pieces.
4. Leave a narrow space of background between pieces if desired.
5. Continue pasting until a design is complete.
6. Dry completely.

VARIATIONS
- Use confetti or holes from a paper punch for the mosaic pieces.
- Use seeds, grain, beans, cereal, or popcorn for mosaic pieces.
- Create a mosaic without a pre-drawn picture for a random or free-form design mosaic.
- Work on wood, rock, or a grocery tray using white glue.
- Create a mosaic from large scraps of paper on a large paper or cardboard base.

LETTER COLLÉ

 A collé is similar to a collage. Scraps of paper are pasted to a background paper to provide decorative additions. In a Letter Collé, letters of the alphabet cut from old magazines are pasted into a design. For instance, a cut-out red capital A could be the hat on a clown. Or an entire design could be made from cut-out M's as birds flying in the sky.

MATERIALS
colorful magazine letters, pre-cut
scissors
paste or glue
paper for the base

PROCESS
1. Place letters on the base paper to create figures, designs, or scenes. Use one alphabet letter in many different styles and prints, or use any number of letters to fit as certain designs and shapes.
2. When satisfied with the design, paste letters to the base paper. However, some artists prefer to paste as they go.

VARIATIONS
*   Add Letter Collé to a drawing or a design. For example, on a drawing of the sea and sky, a capital K on its side might be a boat with an O for the moon. Further drawings could also be added.
*   Paste one letter on a sheet of paper and pass it to a friend to try to draw something using that letter in the drawing.

Magazine Collé

MATERIALS
colorful magazine pictures
scissors
paste or glue
sheet of white paper for the base
crayons or pens

PROCESS
1. Select a magazine picture to be used as texture for a drawing or design. For instance, a magazine picture of a field of wheat could be used as the fur for a lion. Or a magazine picture of a strawberry in a bowl of cereal could be used as the nose of a clown.
2. Cut these magazine pictures into shapes which can create a scene, design, or be part of a drawing.
3. Arrange them on the base paper.
4. When ready, paste down the magazine shapes.
5. Add drawings with crayon or pen to enhance the design if desired.

VARIATIONS
• Paste magazine picture shapes to cover the entire background like a collage.
• Paste magazine picture shapes on paper trying to represent a favorite color or a theme, such as –
  – cut-out flowers pasted to resemble one larger flower
  – red magazine cut-outs to make a Christmas collage
  – blue magazine cut-outs to make a blue collage

 A collé is similar to a collage. Scraps of paper are pasted to a background paper to provide decorative additions. For instance, from a magazine picture of a woman with brown hair, the hair could be cut out and pasted to the collé as brown fields on the farm. A cut-out of a bagel could be pasted to a drawing to be an island in the sea. Although a somewhat abstract idea, artists catch on quickly.

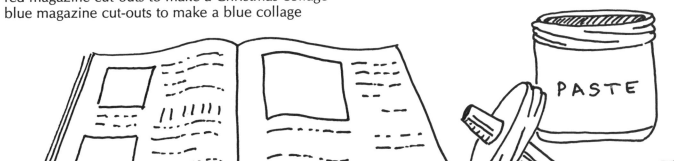

TRACING SHAPERS

 The effect of tracing an object over and over with only a slight movement of the shape each time produces the appearance of something moving quickly before the eyes, like an optical illusion. However, simply tracing shapes and coloring them in is also a good skill and a satisfying activity. It's preferable for each artist to make his or her own tracing shape.

MATERIALS
paper for the base, such as typing paper or copier paper
tape
pencils, crayons, pens
shapes cut from heavier paper
scissors

PROCESS
1. The base paper can be taped to the table to give stability and prevent wiggling.
2. Choose any shape and place it on the paper.
3. Trace around the shape with a drawing tool, holding the shape in place with the non-drawing hand.
4. Next, move the shape slightly and trace again, overlapping the designs.
5. Continue until a desired design has been created.
6. Decorate or color-in the design if desired.

VARIATIONS
- Create Crayon Rubbings, p. 43, by placing the shapes under the paper and rubbing over them with a peeled crayon.
- Use the cut shapes for Chalk Stencils, p. 54.

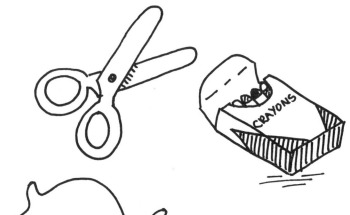

FLIP-AND-SLIDE DESIGN

MATERIALS
construction paper
scissors
glue
base paper in contrasting color

PROCESS
1. From a square of construction paper, cut a shape out of one edge of the square. Save the shape.
2. Cut other shapes out of the other edges of the paper. Save these shapes too.
3. Place the square on the base paper. Glue it in place.
4. Place the shapes back into the spaces from where they were originally cut, like puzzle pieces.

Continue with a flip design or a slide design (below) going to step 5.

FLIP DESIGN
5. Flip the shape over and out of the space, keeping the edges touching. See illustration. Glue in place.
6. Flip and glue the other shapes.
7. Dry.

SLIDE DESIGN
5. Move one of the shapes out of its space slightly, leaving a gap in the puzzle. Glue in place.
6. Slide and glue the other shapes.
7. Dry.

VARIATIONS
- Use unusual papers that will increase the optical illusion.
- Cut a magazine picture into strips and slide them apart slightly. Glue in place.
- Cut a magazine picture in wiggly or zigzag strips. Slide them apart and glue in place.
- Make a crayon rubbing from the design.

 Flip-and-Slides are an optical illusion. The eyes and brain are trying to work together, but the brain thinks it sees something different than it really does.
Experiment with the designs in the illustration or with your own designs and see if the optical illusion happens to your eyes and brain too.

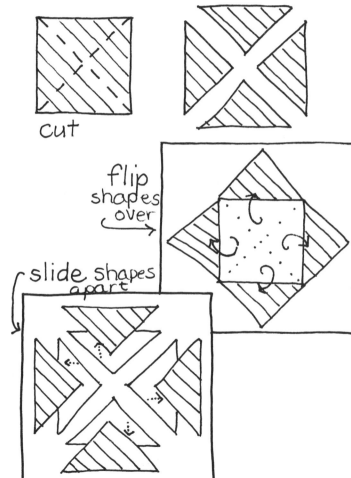

cut

flip shapes over

slide shapes apart

GLUE STICK

PAPER STRIP ART

Long strips of newspaper glued together are versatile and interesting to work with. They can curl, loop, bend, fold, and make interconnecting, unusual designs and sculptures. Prepare the strips first, and begin creating when a supply of strips is ready.

MATERIALS
scissors
long narrow strips of newspaper
glue
tempera paints and brushes
box lid, styrofoam tray, or wood block for the base
straight pins, optional
collage items, optional

PROCESS
1. Cut long narrow strips of newspaper and glue 3 to 4 together to make an even longer strip. Pieces can also be stacked together and glued to make very strong thick strips.
2. Let them dry.
3. Paint with tempera or leave plain.
4. Twist and bend the strips into interlocking shapes.
5. Glue the strips to a base. Use straight pins to hold the sculpture in place, if desired.
6. Decorate the dry sculpture with paints, collage items, or any other ideas if desired.

VARIATIONS
- Thin strips sculpture: twist 3″ paste-coated strips into long ropes, place on foil, and form and pinch them into shapes like fish, stars, animals, and so on. Dry, paint, and mount them on a base.
- Create mobiles.
- Create party decorations like garlands and streamers.

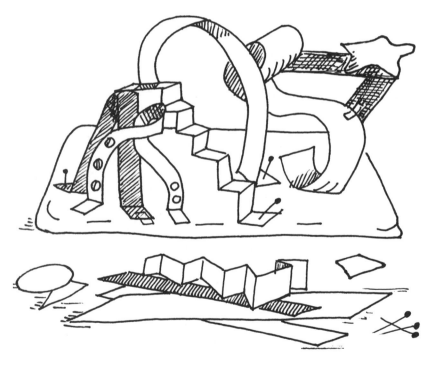

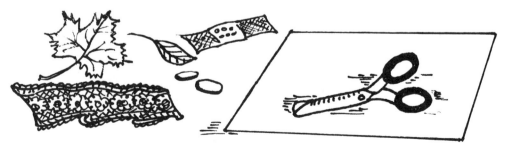

PERFORATED PAPER ART

MATERIALS
perforated strips off the sides of computer paper
liquid starch in several small bowls
powdered vegetable dye colors for each bowl of starch
stick or spoon
rubber or latex gloves, optional
newspaper
glue in dish with paintbrush
matte board, cardboard, or heavy paper plate for the base

When materials like the perforated tear off sides of computer paper are in abundance, why not incorporate them into some creative art? Have an office or school save the perforations from computer paper for this project. The rest is pure art.

PROCESS
1. Mix powdered vegetable dye in a small bowl of liquid starch. Stir with a stick or spoon. Wear rubber gloves or painters' latex gloves to protect hands from staining, if desired. (Artists love to wear painters' or doctors' gloves.)
2. Mix the dye and starch until bright and smooth.
3. Dip perforated strips of computer paper into the bowls of colored starch until coated.
4. Dry the strips completely on newspaper or on a wire.
5. When the strips are dry, glue them in any designs – flat or three dimensional – on the base of matte board or cardboard. The strips can be stacked, joined and expanded, woven, and many other ideas.
6. Dry completely overnight.

VARIATIONS
- Add glitter or confetti to the sticky paper before drying from the dye bath.
- Weave these strips to form multi-colored designs –
    weave them together
    through baskets
    as part of Branch Weaving, p. 131
    any weaving project in this book
- Food coloring can be substituted for powdered vegetable dye.

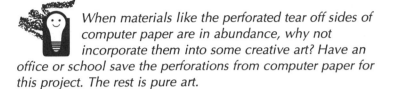

TISSUE BLOSSOMS

 Art tissue has many uses. Creating with the scraps of tissue from other projects makes good sense, and also makes the puffiest, fluffiest creations of all.

MATERIALS
art tissue scraps or squares
white glue in a dish
pencil
sheet of paper for base

PROCESS
1. Push a square or small piece of art tissue around the eraser end of a pencil.
2. Holding the tissue around the eraser with fingertips, dab the tissue into the white glue.
3. Then dab the tissue onto a piece of paper or other base material (matte board, cardboard, poster paper).
4. Dry completely.

HINT
• For a solid color effect, be sure blossoms touch each other with little or no space in between each one.

VARIATIONS
• Fill in blossoms on a pre-drawn design.
• Do a large group project with many hands contributing blossoms.
• For a very large blossom, any types of paper can be pushed around a dowel, can, or jar and dipped into glue in a large bowl or tray. Incorporate cupcake liners for contrast and texture.

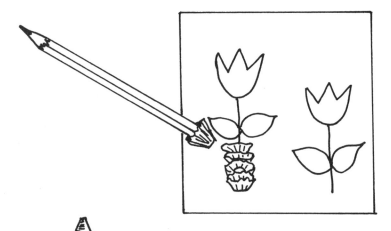

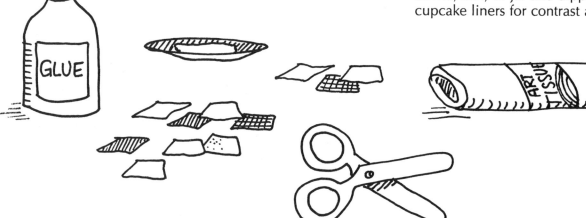

STARCH TISSUE

MATERIALS
art tissue scraps, torn pieces, or squares
liquid starch in a dish
paintbrush
wax paper
black paper, optional
white glue, optional

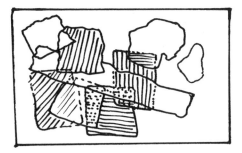

PROCESS
1. Paint liquid starch over a small area of wax paper.
2. Stick a piece of art tissue to the starched area.
3. Paint over the piece with more starch to soak it through and stick all edges to the wax paper.
4. Repeat the steps in 1., 2., and 3.
5. Cover the entire piece of wax paper if desired, overlapping pieces so no wax paper shows through.
6. Dry completely.
7. For a stained glass window look, cut black paper to frame the design, crisscross the design, or to define a silhouette.
8. Stick the frame to the tissue design with white glue.
9. Dry completely. Display in a window to appreciate the colors as light shines through the tissue.

VARIATIONS
- Cut art tissue into shapes, scenes, stories, or figures. Stick to wax paper or plastic wrap with starch or thinned white glue.
- Cut snowflake shapes in different colors of tissue and overlap them, sticking to plastic wrap with liquid starch. Then stick another sheet of plastic wrap over the snowflakes to seal them in between plastic sheets. Cut out and display.
- Cut black paper in the shape of a star, snowflake, or any other shape with "holes" in it. Glue art tissue on the back of the black paper covering the holes. Turn over the design when dry and display in a window.

Liquid starch and art tissue are the perfect combination for an art experience that is extremely easy for all ages as well as bright and aesthetically pleasing. Young artists can easily apply colors and shapes to paper. Older artists may wish to cut the tissue into specific shapes and objects to create a more intricate work. No glue is needed.

Step 7.
Black paper

LIQUID STARCH

FRAMED ARTWORK

Now and then a very special work of art may be saved or given as a gift from the heart to someone special. The artist can choose the artwork, and the rest of this project makes the artwork look very professional and special. Again, it should be the artist's choice.

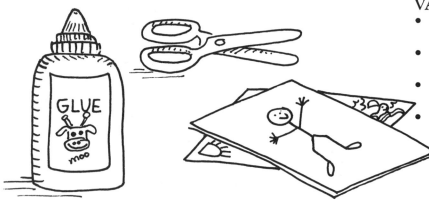

MATERIALS
child's artwork
framing matte scraps from custom frame shop
wood scraps, optional
glue
scissors

PROCESS
1. Go to a local custom picture frame shop and ask for framing matte scraps. One type comes solid in a square or rectangle; the other type comes like a frame with a hole in the center for the artwork. Both are very useful.
   Hint: Leave a box for the shop to save more for you.
2. Select a drawing, painting, or other artwork. If one is not handy, create one!
3. Select one of the matte frame scraps for size and color. Place it around the artwork and see how it looks. Try other frames and colors until you select the one you like the best.
4. Next, glue, tape, or bond the artwork to a solid piece of matte that is about the size of the matte frame and the artwork.
5. Put glue on the back of the frame matte. Press it to the artwork, framing the best parts of the design.
6. Trim any excess design away.
7. For an optional framing idea, glue wood picture frame scraps around the matted artwork. Use pieces the same size as the artwork, or many little pieces for a collage frame.

VARIATIONS
- Find old picture frames at garage sales and thrift shops. Frame artwork in these. Make a wall display with many different sizes and styles of art.
- For a small artwork that is not too heavy, frame as above and add magnetic strips to the back. Stick the artwork to the fridge or other metal area.
- Place magnetic strips on the back of a frame matte. Keep it on the fridge and change the artwork behind it simply by using the magnets.
- Add decoration and design of any kind to the matte frame.

COLOR SPIN

MATERIALS
child's record player (check thrift shops and garage sales)
paper plates with hole punched in center
felt pens
masking tape
scissors
pencil

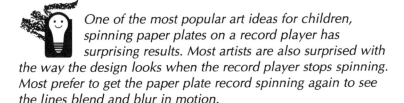

One of the most popular art ideas for children, spinning paper plates on a record player has surprising results. Most artists are also surprised with the way the design looks when the record player stops spinning. Most prefer to get the paper plate record spinning again to see the lines blend and blur in motion.

PROCESS
1. Punch a hole in the center of each paper plate with the point of a scissors or pencil. Observe caution or use adult supervision.
2. Stick a loop of masking tape on the back of the paper plate and place the plate on the record player like a record. The tape will help hold the plate in place.
3. Turn on the record player.
4. Gently touch a felt pen to the spinning plate. Watch the colors move and blend.
5. Experiment with holding the pen still or with moving the pen about on the paper plate.
6. When the design is complete, turn off the record player and remove the plate and the loop of tape.

VARIATIONS
• Cut a shape other than a circle and place it on the record player.
• Experiment with fast and slow speeds on the record player.
• Experiment with different types of pens and coloring tools.
• Build a wooden disk that can spin on a nail, and use squeeze bottles of paint, much like the spinning paint activity at carnivals and fairs.

HINTS
• Tape the arm of the record player to the box of the record player so that it will not be used.
• Tape the electric cord to the table so that no one can pull the record player off the table. Supervise closely.

STUFFED PAPER

Artists enjoy creating things big as life. Stuffed Paper gives the opportunity to create on the large scale, enjoying the process of constructing an artwork that is large but light-weight too.

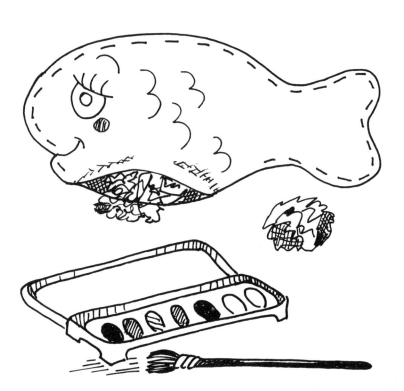

MATERIALS
pencil
large sheet of butcher paper folded in half
scissors
stapler
paint or felt pens
glue, optional
collage items, optional
newspaper
yardstick or ruler, optional
yarn
hole punch

PROCESS
1. Fold a large sheet of butcher paper in half.
2. With the pencil, draw any shape, design, animal, or object. Draw big to fill the butcher paper.
3. Staple two or three staples on each side of the paper to hold for step 4.
4. Cut out the shape through both sheets at the same time. The staples will help keep both sheets together.
5. Paint or decorate the shape with paints, pens, or other items such as sewing trims or other collage items.
6. Dry completely, usually overnight.
7. Next, staple the shapes together, all the way around, but leave an open section big enough for two hands.
8. Begin wadding newspaper up into fluffy balls of paper.
9. Stuff these into the big shape. Push balls all the way into the farthest part of the shape first. Use a ruler or yardstick to help if necessary.
10. When full, staple closed the side left open for stuffing paper.
11. Punch holes in the top of the shape and fit yarn through the holes so that the shape can hang from the ceiling.

VARIATIONS
- Create tropical stuffed fish and hang from the ceiling like they are swimming under water.
- Create a life-size YOU by tracing your body on the paper, decorating it to look like you, and then stapling and stuffing yourself (on the paper, that is).

NEWSPAPER SCULPTURE

MATERIALS
newspaper
masking tape
1/2" wooden dowel (or a pencil or other stick)

PROCESS
TO MAKE THE PAPER ROLLS –
1. Place a sheet of newspaper on the floor.
2. Beginning at a corner, roll the paper around the dowel by rolling diagonally across the paper.
3. Remove the dowel with one hand while holding the roll with the other hand.
4. Tape the end corner of the paper to the roll.
5. Make a large batch of rolls before beginning the sculpture.

TO MAKE THE SCULPTURE –
1. Begin by taping the end of a roll of paper to the floor.
2. Then tape another roll to the first roll. And another, and another, being thoughtful about building a strong structure that won't fall over.
3. Keep adding rolls, bending rolls, sticking a roll inside another roll to make a longer one, and so on.

VARIATIONS
- Build a sculpture that -
can be entered	is a house
moves	is a polyhedron
reaches the ceiling	fills a room
- Add other materials to the sculpture such as feathers, yarn, ribbon, rubber bands, and so on.
- Paint the sculpture upon completion, being sure to cover the floor beneath the sculpture first.
- Use tiny squares of paper and roll them around a drinking straw or pencil to produce a smaller version of the sculpture.
- Use very large rolls of paper made from newsprint from a local newspaper company, rolled around a broomstick for a much larger version of the sculpture.
- For a screamingly fun idea, jump on the sculpture when it is completed and crush it to the ground.

HINTS
- Newspaper Sculpture is an excellent group project.
- Kids will build absolutely huge sculptures.
- This project is fun to do outside.
- Young children sometimes need help tearing masking tape.

 Of all the "build it big" projects, this sculpture is the favorite of all. There is something amazing to children about building something very large very quickly. They also learn in minutes something about engineering and structural strength and balance. The sky is the limit for newspaper sculptures.

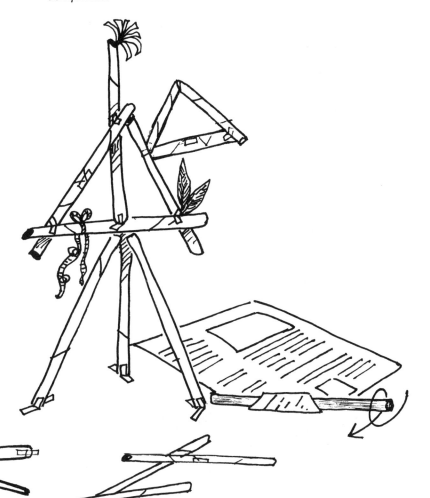

PAPIER-MÂCHÉ PACKAGE

Art experiences would not be complete without working with papier-mâché. Although messy, it is also amazingly versatile and ultimately a strong medium for building large sculptures as well as useful items that last. Preparing for the goo and drips with towels and soapy water will make the clean-up much easier and the activity more enjoyable for all.

MATERIALS

wallpaper paste, buy commercial or use recipe below
any container or package such as –

plastic bottle	waste basket
cardboard box	lampshade
plastic storage container	milk carton
juice container	bowl

scissors
newspaper
paint

PASTE RECIPE

Wallpaper Paste: Mix 2 cups flour and 1/2 cup sugar in a pan. Add enough warm water to make a paste. Then add the rest of 1/2 gallon warm water, stirring. Boil, stirring until thick and clear. Thin with 1/2 quart cold water. Add oil of cinnamon if paste will not be used the same day. Makes about a gallon of paste.

PROCESS

1. Mix the wallpaper paste.
2. Cut or tear strips of newspaper. Soak them in the wallpaper paste briefly, squeezing off the excess paste.
3. Press the paper on a bottle or other container, covering it completely. Cover in several layers if a sturdy result is desired.
4. Dry for several days.
5. Paint.

VARIATIONS

- Decorate a dry container with scrap materials and glue, such as yarn, craft eyes, buttons, and so on.
- Cut a plastic gallon jug in half for a nice bowl.
- Search for discarded plastic things at garage sales and thrift shops for covering with papier-mâché.

CRAYON AND CHALK
chapter 2

FREE DRAWING

 The best thing about free drawing is the freedom to create the unexpected and to discover the bounds of imagination. Experiment with the different artistic effects the following materials and tools have on drawing. Mix and match any combinations.

MATERIALS and PROCESS

1. Provide a variety of paper with differing –
    shapes   colors   textures   thicknesses   absorbencies
2. Challenge drawing by limiting materials to –
    one crayon and one paper color
    one paintbrush, many paints
    colored pencils and tiny paper
    felt pens with opposite colored paper, such as –
        red pen, green paper
        blue pen, yellow paper
3. Experience drawing on paper in different places –

    on the wall   hanging from a string
    on a fence   on the bottom of a table
    at the easel   under a table
    on the floor   inside a dark box
    on a curved surface   under water

4. Experiment with a variety of drawing tools –

    crayons (primary, jumbo, fluorescent, washable)
    peeled crayons   pencils
    Scribble Cookies, p. 47   colored pencils
    flat, shaved crayons   chalk
    crayon stubs   felt pens, fine tip
    candles or paraffin   felt pens, broad tip
    oil pastels   charcoal
    rocks   garden bark
    ink   glue

VARIATIONS

- Add scissors, glue, stapler, tape, stickers to add to the experiment of free drawing.
- Add collage items to the drawing.
- Incorporate magazine pictures, photographs, or cut-outs as part of the drawing.

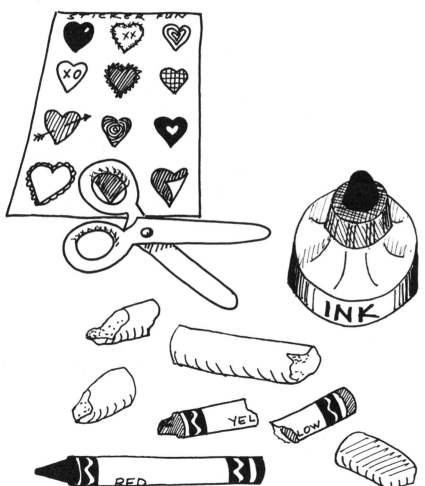

CHALLENGE DRAWING

MATERIALS

Prepare paper with any of the following ideas –
- cut a hole in the paper
- draw a squiggle
- glue on a geometric shape
- draw or glue on a letter

scissors

pens, crayons, or paint

Create the following drawing or painting challenges on paper to either incorporate into a completed drawing or design, or to inspire a new way of drawing.

PROCESS

1. Prepare paper with any of the above challenges to draw on at a table, on the floor, or at the easel. Use any variety of paper sizes, colors, or textures.
2. The artist draws or paints on the paper challenge trying to incorporate the shape, squiggle, hole, or letter into the drawing. Some artists choose to completely ignore or avoid the challenge. Some artists choose to work inside the challenge and leave the rest of the paper blank.
3. As an optional idea, an adult, or a child of writing age (or the artist) can take dictation of the artist's story or comments about the artwork. Writing on the artwork is in addition to the artistic experience.

VARIATIONS

- Artists can create challenges for each other to draw with.
- Sometimes it is challenging to look at a normal drawing and find shapes, letters, and so on that are already a part of the drawing.

ARM DANCING

 Artists draw while music plays, interpreting the music in color or responding to the rhythm in stroke and design. Use large paper and find inspiring music for the most exciting experience in drawing to music.

MATERIALS
large sheet of butcher paper
short, taped musical selection
crayons
paints, optional

PROCESS
1. Place a large sheet of butcher paper on the floor.
2. Play a short musical selection and begin to draw.
3. As the music plays, artists use crayons to "arm dance" on paper. The music might motivate rhythmic drawing movements or expressions of feeling or mood. Some artists like to change colors as the mood of the music changes. Other artists use one color throughout.

VARIATIONS
- Paint instead of draw to music.
- Sculpt with clay to music.
- Use Handful of Scribbles, p. 41, with music.

MUSICAL SUGGESTIONS
- "Hall of the Mountain King" by Peer Gynt
- "Dance of the Sugar Plum Fairy", and other selections from the "Nutcracker Suite" by Tchaikovsky
- any marches by John Phillip Sousa
- "1812 Overture" by Tchaikovsky
- "Claire de Lune" by DeBussy

HANDFUL OF SCRIBBLES

MATERIALS
handful of crayons
rubber band
large sheet of paper
masking tape

PROCESS
1. Wrap a rubber band around a handful of crayons which are all the same length and point size. The tips of all the crayons should be even with each other.
2. Tape a large sheet of paper to the floor, wall, or table.
3. Draw with the handful of crayons experimenting with all the designs and results possible.
4. Change to a clean sheet of large paper and repeat the drawing experience.

VARIATIONS
- Try big arm movements and then very small arm movements.
- Draw with the flat ends of the crayons by turning over the handful of crayons to the opposite end of the bundle.
- Choose specific colors to work with, such as gold and blue crayon on yellow paper. Experiment with other combinations.
- Add some cardboard shapes or other textures under the paper to add surprising designs to the drawing..

 Crayons have many uses and possibilities. A handful of crayons is bundled together with a rubber band and used as one drawing tool with many points of color. Specific colors can be selected by the handful for a more sophisticated art experience, but the fun of a handful of a random selection of colors is effective too.

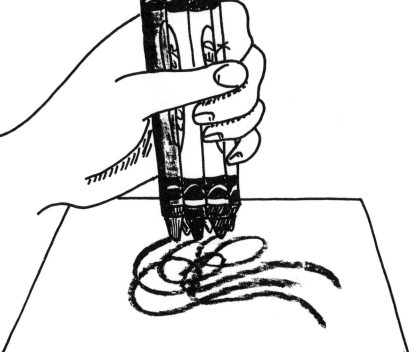

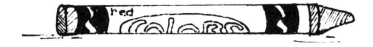

CRAYON ETCHING

 Crayon Etchings can cover an entire sheet of paper, or may be a smaller area within the boundaries of the paper. The idea is to scrape through one layer of crayon to the layers of crayon below, creating a design with scratches and scraps instead of drawing. The layers of coloring take patience and determination so this activity is not for everyone.

MATERIALS
2 or more crayons in contrasting colors
paper
facial tissue or fabric scrap for polishing
sharp scissors
plastic knife
paper clip

PROCESS
1. Cover the entire surface of the paper with a heavy, bright coat of crayon. Avoid dark colors. Create a free or planned design.
2. Color over the bright crayon with dark crayon colors such as black, blue, or violet. Cover all the bright crayon, using pressure and coloring hard.
3. Rub the crayon surface gently with a cloth or tissue to polish and smooth the crayon.
4. Next, scrape the surface of dark crayon with scissor points, a knife, or a paper clip through to the original bright colors.
5. Continue etching the crayon until satisfied with the design.

VARIATIONS
- Experiment with other tools for etching the crayon.
- Work on a warming tray to form two layers of crayon as above. Let the first layer harden and cool. Then add the second layer. When the drawing has cooled again, etch the drawing as described above.
- Etchings may be done with any combination of colors.
- For the second layer, substitute a covering of black or other dark paint. When the paint layer has dried, etch through the paint to the crayon layer.

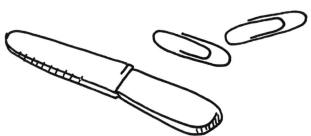

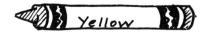

CRAYON RUBBING

MATERIALS
jumbo crayons, peeled (or Scribble Cookies, p. 47)
tape
paper
objects to use for rubbing (see list below)

PROCESS
1. Choose any of the following items to place under the paper, such as –

anything bumpy or textured	leaves
bricks	license plate
cardboard	manhole cover
coins	outdoor and natural items
fence	sidewalk
floor	string
flowers	textured fabrics
gravestone	tree bark
key	wall
keyhole	yarn

2. Place the objects under the paper. Hold the paper with one hand or tape it to the table to keep the paper from wiggling and slipping.
3. Rub the paper with the long flat side of a peeled crayon. Feel for shapes, edges, and items that may have been missed.
4. Continue rubbing with crayon until satisfied with the experience.
5. Remove tape from corners and lift paper from table.

VARIATIONS
*   Place stencils, paper shapes, or other objects on a table. Cover the entire table with a large sheet of butcher paper. Rub the table area with crayons, making rubbings and enjoying the surprise of what appears. This can be provided by someone as a surprise for another, perhaps even as a party activity.
*   Go outside and find things from which to make rubbings.
*   Use charcoal, pencil, or chalk instead of crayon.

 Rubbings have long been a source of beautiful art as well as a way to preserve the history of art from stone carvings, mosaics, and reliefs. Young artists will explore the process of crayon rubbings rather than striving for a finished product. Older artists will achieve more sophisticated results.

CRAYON WAX RESIST

When watery paint is brushed over the crayon drawing, the wax in the crayon resists the paint, which means the paint will not stick to the crayon. However, the paint will adhere to any paper which is showing through or has not been colored with crayon. Painting with a dark color over crayon is particularly effective for a wax resist.

MATERIALS
crayons, many colors
paper
thin tempera paint, watercolors, or ink
paintbrush

PROCESS
1. Draw with crayon on paper making the markings bright and shiny. Any spaces not colored will hold the most paint. Colored areas will resist the paint.
2. Next, wash over the crayon design with a thin dark tempera paint, watercolor paint, or ink.
3. Dry completely. If finished work curls as it dries, place it between two sheets of newspaper and press with an old iron set on low with no steam.

VARIATIONS
- Draw with paraffin or a candle. Then paint over the design as above.
- For an etched effect, scrape through the wax or crayon markings with scissors points before applying the paint wash.
- Scribble big loops and curls of crayon to make a design. Then color-in the loops and shapes. Next wash over the drawing with a dark paint wash.
- Experiment with contrasts in color of paper, crayon, and paint.
- Themes such as "Under the Sea" and "Winter Day" are also effective.

MYSTERY PICTURE

MATERIALS
white crayon, piece of paraffin, or a candle
white paper
watercolor paint or thin tempera paint
soft paintbrush
water

A mystery picture is a rendition of a crayon resist, but has the added fun of the drawing being almost invisible until the paint is applied. Secret messages, secret drawings, and mysterious designs are revealed by the magic of the wax markings resisting the watery paint.

PROCESS
1. Draw a design or picture pressing firmly with white crayon, paraffin, or a candle on white paper. The design will be very hard to see.
2. "Color-in" some areas if desired.
3. Fill the paintbrush with watercolor paint and water.
4. Wash over the paper and observe the drawing appear like magic.

VARIATIONS
- Draw a picture with white crayon and trade with a friend for the watercolor step. Then guess what the picture is as it appears.
- Write secret messages with the Mystery Picture technique.

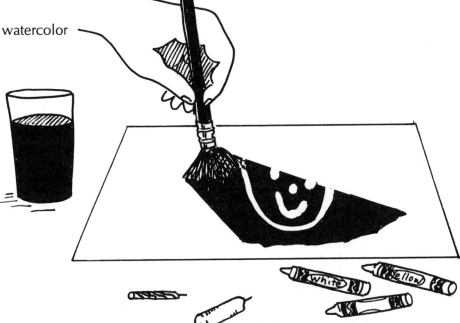

LAMINATIONS

Everyone must have made laminations in elementary school or scout troops at least once. Laminations may have been around as long as wax paper has existed! Artists are fascinated by the melting and changing of crayon and its visibility through the translucent wax paper. Always observe caution around electricity, and then enjoy the timelessness of this basic art experience.

MATERIALS
old crayons
old cheese grater
wax paper
newspaper
old iron
yarn
scissors

PROCESS
1. Grate crayon onto a sheet of wax paper.
2. Cover this with a second sheet of wax paper. If this project will hang in a window when complete, insert a piece of yarn between the wax papers now, letting the end hang out of the papers.
3. Cover the wax papers and crayon shavings with newspaper to absorb any spills or leaks.
4. With a warm iron, quickly press down on the covered wax paper and shavings. Too hot or too much pressure will muddy the design, so start gently and peek often to see the results.
5. When satisfied with the melting, remove the newspaper.
6. Trim the edges of the lamination if desired, or cut the lamination into any shape.
7. Hang in a window if desired.

VARIATIONS
• Create laminations in small wax paper sandwich bags for the easiest approach of all.
• Laminations can be created in long banner style shapes, circles, flowers, or any shape at all.
• Include leaves, yarn, doilies, stickers, cut-outs, confetti, sand, glitter, art tissue, or other bits and scraps of things in the lamination.
• Mount the lamination between paper frames or tape to a framing matte.
• Use dry pressed flowers, leaves, or seaweed between the wax papers with or without the crayon shavings.
• Create a similar project between sheets of clear contact paper, but do not iron.
• Create a similar project between sheets of clear plastic wrap with liquid starch to bind them. Again, do not iron.

SCRIBBLE COOKIES

MATERIALS
old crayon stubs, peeled and broken
old muffin tin
warm oven
oven mitt
freezer

PROCESS
1. Save stub ends of old crayons.
2. Peel and break the crayons into pieces.
3. Sort colors into an old muffin tin, one color per cup. Or mix colors in each cup to make rainbow swirled scribble cookies.
4. Place the muffin tin in the warm oven which has been turned off.
5. Keep an eye on the melting crayons, and remove them from the oven when they just turn squishy but not totally liquid. Use an oven mitt and adult help.
6. Next, for quickest and easiest removal of scribble cookies, place the muffin tin in the freezer for about a half hour.
7. Remove from the freezer, and POP! out.

HINTS
- Kids love metallic colors such as gold, silver, and copper. These colors are available in bulk at school supply stores.
- Assign this muffin tin to crayon melting from now on and avoid cleaning the wax from its surface. Muffin tins come in handy for many crayon melting art ideas. However, the muffin tin will wash in very hot soapy water if you must return it to baking use.

VARIATIONS
- Color with scribble cookies as you would any crayon.
- Use scribble cookies for –

encaustic painting, p. 49	embossing
rubbings, p. 43	etching, p. 42
scribbling	arm dancing, p. 40
laminations, p. 46	crayon resist, p. 44

Saving old crayons has finally found a use that has amazing art properties for all ages. You may find yourself breaking and peeling brand new crayons just because it's so much fun to create these melted crayon disks for coloring, drawing, and rubbings.

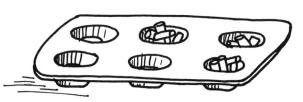

WARMED CRAYON

Warm, smooth, fragrant melted crayons seem to have a calming effect on even the most active artists.
Drawing on a heated tray causes the crayons to melt as the drawing progresses, leaving an artwork that changes the appearance of the paper to seem waxy and translucent.

MATERIALS
electric warming tray, set on low or med/low
aluminum foil, optional
peeled crayons
paper (bond or copier paper works well)
oven mitt or thick work gloves
newspaper for drying artwork

PROCESS
1. Locate a warming tray from a thrift shop or garage sale. They are inexpensive and have many uses.
2. Cover the warming tray with foil, if desired. This makes clean up easy, but is not necessary. Tray will wipe clean with a rag or paper towel if the tray is still warm.
3. Wear an oven mitt or old work glove on the non-drawing hand for holding the paper or steadying against the warming tray.
4. Two melting techniques -
   a. Place a sheet of paper directly on the foil, holding it in place with the gloved non-drawing hand. Draw on the warmed paper with the crayons. Draw slowly so the crayon can melt while drawing.
   b. Draw directly on the clean foil. When a melted design is complete, press a sheet of paper against the melted design. Then lift the paper off by the corner and a print of the melted design will have transferred to the paper.
5. Hang the cooled design in a window if desired, or hold up to the light to see the light shine through the wax.
6. Wipe the tray with a rag or towel while it is still warm.

HINTS
* Observe safety around electric appliances:
  - one child at a time working at the warming tray
  - hold the crayon at the end away from the heat with the drawing hand
  - wear an oven mitt on the non-drawing hand, or both hands
  - watch that the electric cord does not stretch across traffic
  - tape the cord to the table for extra caution

VARIATIONS
* Draw on a paper plate which has been placed in a foil-lined electric fry pan set on low heat.
* Draw on fabric which has been stretched across and taped to the warming tray.
* Create little designs on folded note paper for greeting cards.
* Cut designs from paper and glue to a different background.

ENCAUSTIC PAINTING

MATERIALS
warming tray or electric frying pan
aluminum foil
old muffin tin
crayon stubs, peeled and broken
old paintbrushes
paper

When crayon is melted to liquid form, the colors may be painted on paper with a paintbrush, reacting somewhat like a thick paint. The melted crayon dries and hardens as it is brushed on the paper, resembling the look of an oil painting. As with all projects involving heat and children, observe caution and safety.

PROCESS
1. Sort crayon stubs into muffin tin cups by color.
2. Cover the warming tray or electric frying pan with aluminum foil to protect the surface from crayon.
3. Set the muffin tin on the warming tray with the heat set on low. If low does not melt the crayon, increase heat to a comfortable setting.
4. When the crayon has melted to a completely liquid state, dip an old paintbrush into the crayon and paint directly on paper. The crayon dries quickly on the paper, so keep dipping the brush in the melted crayon to keep it soft and full of color.
5. Dry the completed artwork for a few minutes.

HINTS
- If the crayon cools or hardens in the tin, re-heat and melt. The same holds true for the paintbrushes. If the crayon hardens in the brush, dip the brush into warm melted crayon until the wax on the brush melts again.
- The muffin tin and brushes should be assigned to melted crayon work from now on as cleaning them for other uses is difficult.
- Tape the paper down for extra security.
- Brace tray or pan to prevent tipping or spilling, and be sure cord is out of the way of traffic or elbows.

VARIATIONS
- Paint with melted crayon on rocks, wood, matte board, or other surfaces of choice.
- Mix colors on the paper.
- Experiment with creating new colors by mixing crayons in the muffin tin cups and then melting.

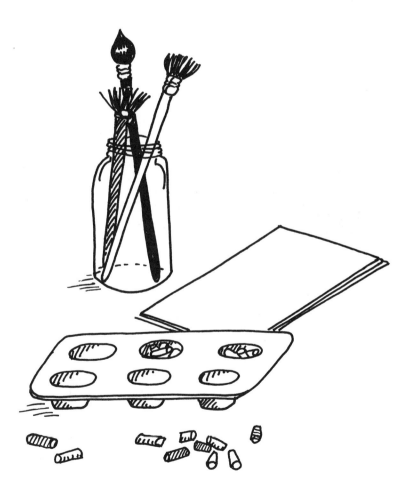

FABRIC TRANSFER

 Fabric crayons are available at most stores in the school supply section, and at all hobby stores. The results are bright and permanent, and a fascinating process for artists. I have pillow cases, a quilt, and a T-shirt that have been washed and dried over and over again for years, and have retained the same bright design.

MATERIALS
fabric crayons
washed 100% cotton fabric
plain white paper
old iron
old towel or newsprint
table or ironing board

PROCESS
1. Cover a table with a thick towel and a sheet of newsprint, or cover an ironing board with a sheet of newsprint. Heat the iron to cotton setting, no steam.
2. Draw on white paper with fabric crayons. Remember if writing words or names to write them backwards so that the transfer will be frontwards.
3. Place the drawing face side down on the fabric.
4. Cover the drawing with another piece of newsprint.
5. Press firmly with a hot, dry iron. Also, follow the directions on the fabric crayon box for other hints and suggestions.
6. Peel away the paper drawing from the fabric. A bright transfer on the drawing will be printed on the fabric.

VARIATIONS
* Some fabric crayon transfer ideas are –

applique	gift bag	puffy picture frame
apron	head band	quilt square
back pack	kite	T-shirt
bandana	pillow	tote bag
belt	pillow case	windsock

* Frame a fabric transfer design with an embroidery hoop. Display on the wall.

ART GALLERY

MATERIALS
2 pieces of matte board, 8"x 8", for the covers
matte board, 8"x 8" pieces for any number of pages
masking tape or cloth library tape
crayons, pens

 The pages of the art gallery are like a book which folds out in a long, continuous display from front to back. It can tell a story, become a cluster of connected ideas, or simply display a collection of artwork.

PROCESS
1. Draw a series of pictures or designs on the squares of matte board.
2. Tape the matte boards together with masking tape or library cloth tape so that the pages fold in an accordion style. It helps to leave a small gap between the boards when the tape is applied. The tape will cover the gap.
3. Decorate the matte board covers and tape them to the other drawing boards, one at the beginning and one at the end. A title, other ideas in words, or a story may also be written on the covers or on the pages.
4. Fold the gallery into a book shape, or display the opened gallery on a table or shelf.

VARIATIONS
• Draw pictures in a story or cluster of connected ideas.
• Draw pictures or designs around a theme or topic.
• Cut out shapes from paper or wallpaper scraps and paste the shapes on each matte board instead of drawing.
• Illustrate a favorite story or tale.
• Collect favorite artworks and paste them to the matte boards to build a collection of favorites.

WET PAPER CHALK

 The normal dusty, dull qualities of chalk are changed by the chalk particles absorbing the water, making the chalk brighter and less smudgy. For even brighter chalk drawings, soak the chalk in sugar-water for ten minutes which will also reduce smearing.

MATERIALS
heavy paper
water
sponge
colored chalk

PROCESS
1. Dampen heavy paper with a sponge soaked with water.
2. Draw over the damp paper with chalk.
3. Dry completely.

VARIATIONS
*   To reduce smearing further, an adult may spray the chalk drawing outside with a fixative such as hairspray, clear enamel, or a polymer spray.
*   Draw on a wet sponge with chalk and then press or draw with the sponge on dry paper.

BRUSHED CHALK

MATERIALS
colored chalk
papers in light colors
cotton balls and facial tissues
scraps of construction paper

PROCESS
BRUSHING DESIGN –
1. The first technique is to draw with chalk on paper and then brush or rub the marks with a cotton ball or facial tissue. This makes a blurred, blended design.
2. Use a second color next to the first color and brush the two colors together to create a new color.

STENCIL DESIGN –
1. Tear scrap paper into any shapes or pieces.
2. Rub chalk on the edge of the torn shape.
3. Place the chalked shape on a light piece of paper and hold it with the non-drawing hand.
4. Brush the chalk from the edge of the torn paper shape and out onto the light colored construction paper with a cotton ball or piece of facial tissue.
5. Remove the shape to see the remaining design on the paper.

HINTS
• Artists tend to want to use a new cotton ball or tissue for each brushing. Encourage one piece for the entire creation.
• Chalky hands, fingers, and clothes are to be expected. Plan ahead by having towels and warm, soapy water available and cover artists with aprons if necessary.

VARIATIONS
• Experiment with Brushed Chalk on textured paper, white cardboard, and with rubbings (like crayon rubbings).
• Make a design by repeating the same shape in a pattern over and over on the paper.

 Chalk has the unusual and artistic quality of being powdery, and thereby able to blur, blend, and smudge. One way to mix and enjoy chalk colors is to brush the chalk with a cotton ball or facial tissue, softening and mixing colors on the paper.

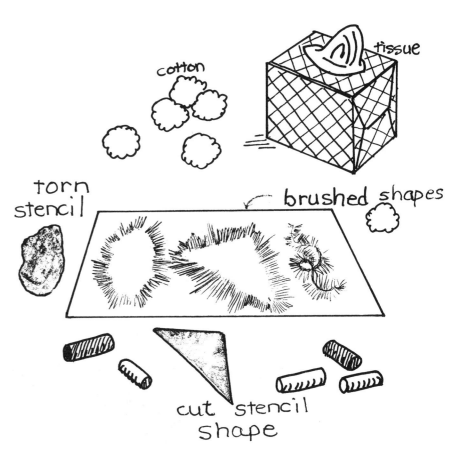

cotton

tissue

torn stencil

brushed shapes

cut stencil shape

CHALK STENCILS

cut out
shape

Creating stencils with colored chalk is an art technique with a magical quality as the stencil designs change before the eyes. Although the directions are somewhat more involved than for many other chalk ideas, the beauty and magic are worth the effort.

MATERIALS
squares of heavy paper, such as old file folders
scissors
colored chalk
paper in light colors
facial tissues or cotton balls

PROCESS
1. Cut any shape from a folded square of heavy paper. Keep the shape and the paper from around the shape too. Both can be used as stencils with entirely different art results.
2. Place a stencil (either piece) on the paper.
3. Trace around the shape (or trace inside the opposite piece).
4. Without removing the stencil, hold the stencil with the non-drawing hand and at the same time, take a piece of tissue or a cotton ball in the drawing hand.
5. Brush the chalk outline gently with the tissue or cotton, brushing out and away from the shape (or brushing in and filling the opposite piece).
6. Remove the stencil. The effect will be soft and muted with a distinct stencil design with clean edges.
7. Repeat as desired.

HINT
• The stencil must be held still and not removed before brushing the marks for this art technique to work. However, if the artist decides on a different idea or moves the stencil, this too is acceptable and effective chalk art.

VARIATIONS
• Create repetitive patterns with stencils and chalk.
• Overlap stencils and designs for a mixing of colors and shapes. Experiment with a variety of colors overlapping and blending.
• Find objects to use as stencils, such as a soup can, shoe, comb, hammer, or other ideas.

PAINTED CHALK

MATERIALS
colored chalk
2 tablespoons thick white tempera paint
jar lid
black or dark paper

 By dipping colored chalk into white tempera paint, the chalk takes on a new property of outlining itself in white when drawn on paper. Chalk can also be dipped into other colors.

PROCESS
1. Dip the end of a piece of colored chalk into some thick white tempera in a jar lid.
2. Draw with the whitened, moist chalk. The marks will show the distinct color of the chalk edged with white against dark paper.

VARIATIONS
- Experiment with dipping the chalk in black paint and then drawing on white paper. Try other color combinations too.
- Create a sampler of strokes and markings such as –
zigzags	straights
spirals	curves
dots	letters
- Draw with chalk on paper. Brush another paper with white tempera, and then press the chalk drawing face down into the wet painted paper. Lift off the drawing and see the print.

 Dipping chalk into liquid starch enhances the brightness of the drawing and also helps the chalk marks resist smudging. However, all chalk will smudge, which is part of the beauty and the versatility of the medium, and part of the mess too.

MATERIALS
colored chalk
liquid starch in a cup
paper or matte board for the base

PROCESS
1. Dip the end of the chalk into a cup of liquid starch.
2. Draw with the chalk on the paper, just like with a crayon.
3. Continue dipping and drawing.
4. Dry completely.

VARIATIONS
- For a shiny chalk drawing, dip chalk into sweetened condensed milk.
- Substitute a mixture of sugar and water for the liquid starch for the same results as starch.
- Draw with chalk on black matte board for a neon look.
- Experiment with chalk on a variety of papers, especially papers with texture.

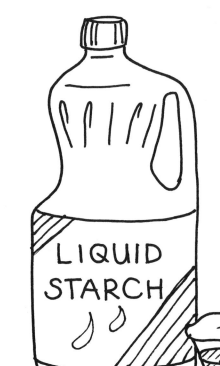

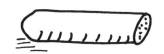

CRUSHED CHALK

MATERIALS
colored chalk
water in dish
paintbrushes
rock
wax paper or paper plate
muffin tin or other small containers for crushed chalk

 Painting with chalk is an unusual idea accomplished by crushing the chalk to powder and then using a wet paintbrush to apply the powder to paper. The beauty of the chalk powder is that the colors will mix and blend during the painting offering a surprise of many new colors.

PROCESS
1. Crush chalk with a rock on a paper plate or wax paper. Do not pound the chalk. Press the rock gently but firmly against the chalk until it crushes to powder.
2. Slip the powdered chalk into a small container such as the cups of a muffin tin.
3. Crush more colors and prepare more cups of powder.
4. When there are several colors ready, dip a small paintbrush into water, and then dip it into the powdered chalk.
5. Next, apply the wet powdered chalk to paper, painting with the chalk.
6. Dry completely.

VARIATIONS
- Dip a paintbrush into liquid starch and then into crushed chalk. Paint on paper.
- Paint with small pieces of wet sponge.
- Dip a finger in water and then in chalk.
- Mix and blend colors on the paper.
- Experiment with mixing different colors of crushed chalk in the muffin cups.

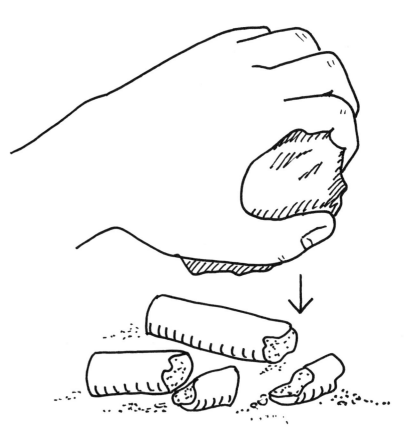

SPONGE CHALK

 Chalk has always been a favorite medium for artists young and old. Making a chalk print is easy and effective when a drawing is made on a flat wet sponge and then pressed onto a piece of paper.

MATERIALS
flat sponges
water in a baking pan
colored chalk
paper
towels to dry hands

PROCESS
1. Dip a flat sponge into a pan of water and wring out. Dry hands if necessary.
2. Draw with chalk on the wet sponge.
3. Then press the sponge onto a piece of paper to make a chalk print. Several prints will be possible from one drawing.
4. Re-draw over the same design on the sponge to make the same print over and over. Or, rinse the sponge and make a new drawing.

VARIATIONS
- Draw on little pieces of wet sponge and make chalk prints.
- Crush chalk into powder and dip a wet sponge or brush into the powder. Use like paint.
- Experiment with different colors of paper. Black paper is often effective with bright chalk colors.

PAINT AND DYE

chapter 3

EXPERIPAINT

Many different materials and tools can be used to paint with, and just as many materials can be painted on. The challenge and experience of "experipainting" is trying as many combinations as possible without concern as to how the art project will turn out. The success of experipainting is in the process and experimenting, not the end product.

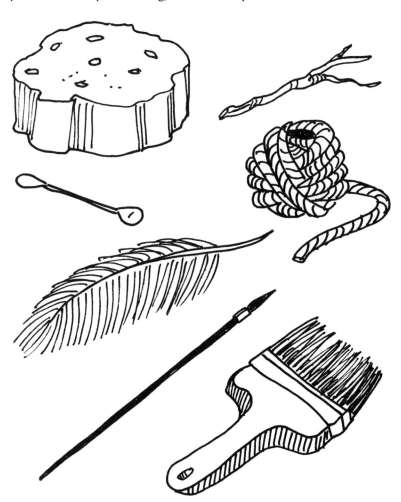

MATERIALS and PROCESS
Experiment with techniques, tools, and surfaces, such as –

TECHNIQUES
    dry paints on wet paper
    wet paint on wet paper
    melt crayon to use as paint
    bold and heavy paint
    light and delicate paint
    thick or thin paint
    powdered paint
    whipped paint
    salty paint

PAPERS	OTHER SURFACES	PAINTING TOOLS	
absorbent	brick	berry basket	hand, foot, elbow
bumpy	cardboard	broom	junk
crumpled	cookie sheet	bubbles	lips, nose, chin
folded	fabric	clay	plunger
fuzzy	foil	corn cob	potato
glazed	leaf	cotton ball	roll-on bottle
rolled	Plexiglas	cotton swab	rubber band
scored	rock	duster	sponge
smooth	tile	eraser	spool
torn	wall	feather	stick
with holes	window	fingers	string
wrinkled	wood	foil	toy car
transparent	snow	gadgets	wood scraps

MIX INGREDIENTS WITH PAINT
coffee grounds	glue	sand
cornstarch	ice	shampoo
corn syrup	milk	soap
flour	rain	spices
glitter	salt	starch

Paint, experiment, create, explore. Let the imagination soar. Feel free to throw away or save paint experiments.

DAMP PAPER PAINT

MATERIALS
water
flat pan
butcher paper cut to fit flat pan
paint (watercolor, tempera, or food coloring)
paintbrushes
jars of water
paper towels
newspaper

Painting on wet paper causes the water to thin the paint, producing a soft, blurred, blended effect. The painting experience itself has a gentle, calm quality. Use a soft touch and observe the paints flowing and blurring into the water.

PROCESS
1. Fill a flat pan with water and place the sheet of paper in the pan to moisten. Remove.
2. Place the paper on a table while still wet.
3. Use a paper towel to blot off some excess moisture, but keep the paper shiny and wet.
4. Paint on the wet paper. Experiment with dripping, swirling, mixing colors on the paper, and blending.
5. Leave on the table to dry, or place the painting on a dry sheet of newspaper and carry to a drying area.

VARIATIONS
- To moisten paper:
  - wash over the paper with a big brush full of water
  - fill a sponge with water and dampen paper
  - hold the paper under the faucet and cover with water
- Experiment with a variety of papers such as:
  - grocery bag
  - textured paper
- For a batik effect, crumple the wet paper and then spread it out on a table and paint on the paper as usual.

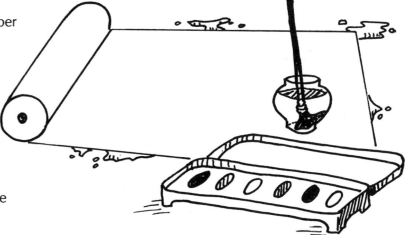

MARKING PEN PAINT

Painting with water over marks made from waterbased felt pens is similar to techniques used in "paint with water" books found next to the coloring books in grocery stores. In this art experience, the picture or design is created by the individual artist's imagination and not by an adult commercial artist.

MATERIALS
waterbased felt pens
any smooth, heavy paper such as –
    heavy drawing paper
    fingerpaint paper
    tag board
    posterboard
water in a jar
soft paintbrushes, 1 fine and 1 broad

PROCESS
1. Draw with felt pen.
2. Using a wet paintbrush, paint over the felt pen marks. Fresh felt pen marks paint better than very dry ones, so use the wet paintbrush frequently instead of waiting until the entire drawing is completed.

VARIATIONS
- Draw with felt pens on wet paper.
- Draw around stencil shapes and designs with felt pen and then paint the lines with water.
- Make greeting cards or wrapping paper.
- Paint the finished dry drawing with watercolors to add more color and design.
- Press pieces of clear contact paper on the paper before beginning the painting. Draw and paint. Then carefully peel the contact paper pieces away, leaving stenciled shapes and designs.

MASKING TAPE RESIST

MATERIALS
masking tape
scissors
paper
watercolor paint
paintbrush
water in a jar

 When areas of the paper are covered by masking tape, the paint leaves that part of the painting blank or the color of the paper. Once the technique is understood, a long list of other creative possibilities will emerge from the artist.

PROCESS
TECHNIQUE 1 –
1. Tear or cut pieces of masking tape and stick them to the paper. Press gently so that the tape can be removed later.
2. Paint over the masking tape pieces and onto the paper.
3. Let the painting dry.
4. When dry, carefully peel off the pieces of masking tape to reveal the stenciled, unpainted areas underneath.

TECHNIQUE 2 –
1. Follow step one above. Cover most of the paper with tape shapes and pieces.
2. Using a light colored paint or a thinned color, paint over the tape pieces.
3. Next, remove some of the pieces, but not all of them.
4. Paint over the newly exposed areas and anywhere else with a slightly darker paint or slightly thicker paint color.
5. Remove a few more pieces of tape. Paint again with a still darker or thicker paint color.
6. Continue the paint layering process until no pieces of tape remain.

VARIATIONS
- Create masking tape resist on commercial wrapping paper or a used poster. It may be necessary to use tempera paint instead of watercolor paint.
- Print words, messages, or signs with masking tape. Paint over the tape and onto the paper and then remove the tape.

SALT PAINTING

This salt mixture creates a crystallized painting as the artwork dries. Make several cups of salt paint in different colors for a rainbow of crystal colors.

MATERIALS
liquid starch
paper plate, matte board, or cardboard
water
tempera paint or food coloring
paintbrushes
salt

PROCESS
1. Mix the following in a cup –
   1/8 cup liquid starch
   1/8 cup water
   1 tablespoon tempera paint (or 2 squirts food coloring)
   1/2 cup table salt
2. Mix several cups of different colors.
3. Apply the mixture to the paper or board with a paintbrush. Stir the mixture often while painting.
4. The painting will crystallize as it dries.

VARIATIONS
- Salt Painting is effective for winter and snow designs.
- Mix Epsom salt into the paint for crystals shaped differently than table salt crystals.

SALTY WATERCOLOR

MATERIALS
white glue in a squeeze bottle
watercolor paint
paintbrush
jar of water
matte board or cardboard
bag of salt poured into a plastic tub (big enough for a sheet of paper to lay flat)

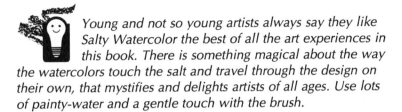

Young and not so young artists always say they like Salty Watercolor the best of all the art experiences in this book. There is something magical about the way the watercolors touch the salt and travel through the design on their own, that mystifies and delights artists of all ages. Use lots of painty-water and a gentle touch with the brush.

PROCESS
1. Draw a design with white glue on matte board. Use lots of glue and thick lines.
2. Place the glue drawing in the tub of salt and use your hands to pour salt over the drawing. Lift and tilt the design while still in the tub so that the salt will fall back into the tub.
3. Return to the table with the glue and salt design.
4. Fill a paintbrush with lots of water and paint.
5. Gently touch the tip of the soaking brush to the salt and let the paint absorb into the salt and travel into the design. Try not to "paint" or scrub with the paintbrush into the glue and salt.
6. Rinse the brush in clear water and continue painting.
7. Dry the design completely.

HINTS
- Matte board is the suggested base paper because it will not bend and thereby crack the dried salt drawing.
- Because the salt tends to flake and fall off after time, wrap the design with clear plastic and tape it to the back of the matte board to protect the artwork.

VARIATIONS
- Create a Salty Watercolor on a block of wood, rock, styrofoam grocery tray, or fabric stretched over cardboard.
- Brush glue with a paintbrush on the matte board for a variety of line widths and thicknesses. Then add the salt and watercolor paint.

FUNNY PAINTS

The following recipes for paints are used on paper or other surfaces. Each one adds a new dimension to the properties of tempera paint. All require little or no extra expense and can actually extend the life and quantity of tempera paint over the long term.

MATERIALS

Mix liquid or powdered tempera paints to any desired consistency with one of the following ingredients. Add some water to the paint if it seems too thick.

- white glue – for shiny paint
- liquid starch – for smooth, translucent paint
- sweetened condensed milk – for a glazed, shiny paint
- egg yolk – for bright, sticky, glossy paint
- cornstarch – for a hard, porcelain quality paint
- paste – for thick, textured frosting-like painting
- whipped soap flakes – for very thick billowy painting
- baby oil — for a paint that will not dry (no water)
- corn syrup – for a glossy, sticky paint (no water)
- shampoo – whip with paint until fluffy, airy

bowls or cups for mixing paint   paintbrushes, craft sticks
spoon or stick   jar of water for rinsing
paper, cardboard, or other base

PROCESS

1. Mix tempera paint, liquid or powdered, with one of the ingredients above. For example, pour white glue into a cup and add tempera paint, stirring with a paintbrush. A little water may be added to thin very thick paint.
2. Paint as with any paint on paper. For very thick paint recipes, spread the paint like frosting with a craft stick, spoon, or stick. Experiment with squeezing the paint from a bottle or cake decorating bag.
3. Dry the artwork completely.
4. Keep experimenting with mixtures.

HINT

- Keep in mind that this activity and the recipes are discovery experiments. Results will vary.

VARIATIONS

- When a painting is completely dry, coat the entire work with white glue thinned with water for a layer of clear glaze. Dry overnight.
- Paint pine cones, rocks, driftwood, glass, and other materials and surfaces.
- Paint with a sponge brush from a hardware store for a smooth finish.
- To help paint adhere to a shiny, smooth surface such as foil or plastic, add a few drops of dishwashing detergent to the paint mixture.

VEGETABLE DYE PAINT

MATERIALS
1/8 teaspoon vegetable dye powder
1 tablespoon water
liquid starch
container
stirring stick

PROCESS
1. Dissolve 1/8 teaspoon dye powder in 1 tablespoon of water.
2. Mix the dissolved dye with liquid starch to the amount desired, about a pint for a bright color. Adjust dye or starch for paler or brighter colors.
3. Paint as with any paint.

VARIATIONS
- For the most brilliant paint, mix vegetable dye powder with wallpaper paste or craft paste.
- Make the cornstarch mixture found in Chapter 7, p. 148, and mix with vegetable dye powder.

HINTS
- Vegetable dye paint does not cover lettering on boxes or newspaper like opaque tempera paint. It has a transparent quality that works well for paintings.

 Vegetable coloring comes in a highly concentrated powder form that can be used as a dye or a paint. It is costly and has to be bought in bulk, but one pound of color will last a school for several years and a home for generations. One of the best things about powdered vegetable dye is that it comes in an array of glorious colors. Vegetable dye is available at school supply stores; it is similar to food coloring but is brighter and can be substituted with food coloring for any art idea. It is sometimes called Edicol.

DRIP AND RUN

Thin paint will run and drip on paper that is tipped and tilted. The running paint will form tracks and trails that cause other drips and puddles of paint to join in. Using more than one color will bring about colors that mix, blend, and cross over each other.

MATERIALS
thin tempera paints
cups
paintbrush, spoon
heavy paper, smooth matte board, or paper plate

PROCESS
1. Mix tempera paint with water in a cup until thin and runny. Make several cups of color if desired.
2. With a spoon or paintbrush, drip a spot or puddle of paint on the paper.
3. Tip and turn the paper this way and that, letting the paint run in different directions. Add more than one color and the colors of paint will drip and run across each other, making new shades and trails or paths of paint.
4. Dry the artwork completely.

HINT
- Place the heavy paper in a tray which has sides to contain drips on the tray and not on the floor.

VARIATIONS
- Apply paint to paper by dipping a straw into paint and holding the dry end with a finger, holding the paint in the straw. Release the paint on the paper by releasing the finger.
- Change colors often to experiment with the mixing of colors as they cross and mix with each other.
- Working outdoors, fill a turkey baster with paint and squirt the paint on a large piece of cardboard or paper taped to a piece of cardboard. Tip the board to run the colors together.
- Paint with thin tempera paint onto a sheet of paper taped to the wall or to a fence. Protect the floor underneath the work. Paint will drip and run down throughout the design.

TEMPERA PAINT

SQUEEZING PAINT

MATERIALS
empty squeeze containers such as –
    ketchup
    mustard
    liquid hand soap
    shampoo
    dish detergent
tempera paints
sheets of paper, medium or large size

Any time a new way of painting is tried, the understanding of what paint and paint tools are capable of accomplishing or causing grows. The effects of squeezing paint are completely different than using a paintbrush, and open many new possibilities for creativity.

PROCESS
1. Fill empty squeeze containers with tempera paints.
2. Squeeze the paint on to the paper. Use gentle pressure. Move the opening of the container about, drawing or making designs.
3. Dry the painting or design completely.

VARIATIONS
- Squeezing color is effective on a very large surface or even on a vertical surface such as a wall. Prepare for dripping and excitement. Remember gentle squeezing works the best. Good luck!
- Squeeze paint from a turkey baster onto a large paper surface outside on the grass.
- Add other painting tools to this activity such as –

brush	stick	straw
swab	plastic knife	spoon
sponge	bamboo skewer	hands

PULLED STRING

Pulling paint-soaked string from between a folded sheet of paper creates intriguing designs and mixtures of colors. Sometimes younger artists need help controlling the string and paper, but all results are impressive.

MATERIALS
yarn or string in 1 foot lengths
tempera paint in a styrofoam tray, taped to a table top
shallow dish
paper folded in half

PROCESS
1. Place a pre-folded sheet of paper on the table beside the tray filled with paint.
2. Hold one end of the string, and drop the rest of the string into the paint, keeping hold of the dry end.
3. Pull the string out of the paint and place it on one half of the opened sheet of paper. Keep the dry end of the string hanging off the edge of the paper.
4. While still holding the string, fold the paper over on top of the paint-soaked string. Use the free hand to do the folding.
5. Next, press down on the paper with the free hand and pull the string out with the string hand. Open the paper and look at the design.
6. Repeat the steps above with a new color and a separate string. Use a separate string for each color.
7. When satisfied with the paint design, dry completely with the paper open, not folded.

VARIATIONS
- Try using thick or thin paint.
- Try using thick or thin strings.
- Mix glue with the paint for a different effect.
- Cut out the designs when dry.

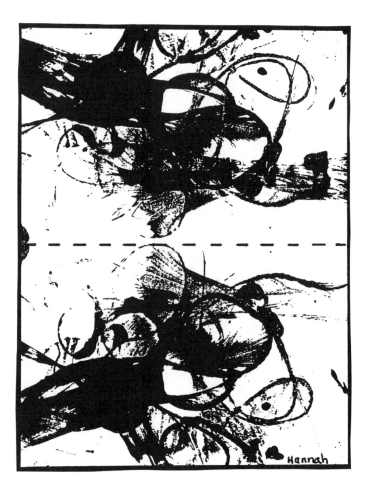

BLOTTOS

MATERIALS
tempera paints in cups
spoon or paintbrush for each cup
large sheet of butcher paper, or any paper

PROCESS
1. Fold the paper in half. Open it.
2. Spoon or brush drops and blobs of paint on the paper. Place paint on the fold line for an effective Blotto.
3. Refold the paper.
4. With the palm of the hand, press and rub the paper from the fold out to the edge of the paper.
5. Open the paper and observe the design. Dry completely.

VARIATIONS
- When the painting is dry, cut out the design. Glue on a contrasting colored background or hang on the wall.
- Create butterflies, bugs, or alien creatures. Add other effects or characteristics with black felt pens or paint.
- Place the paint on the paper trying to create shapes or designs such as a heart, flower, bug, or other symmetrical design. Place half the design on half the paper. When it is folded, the other half of the design will be repeated forming one whole design with a fold in the middle.
- Read the book, It Looks Like Spilled Milk for ideas about what Blotto shapes can look like to different people. Then create "spilled milkblottos" with white paint on blue paper.
- Imagine what the Blotto resembles and what interesting shapes, people, animals, or stories can be seen in the paint design.

 By placing paint between sheets of paper and then folding them together, colors mix and form strange and interesting shapes. Shapes often resemble butterflies because of the symmetry, but a butterfly shape need not be the goal. Enjoy the surprise of color and design.

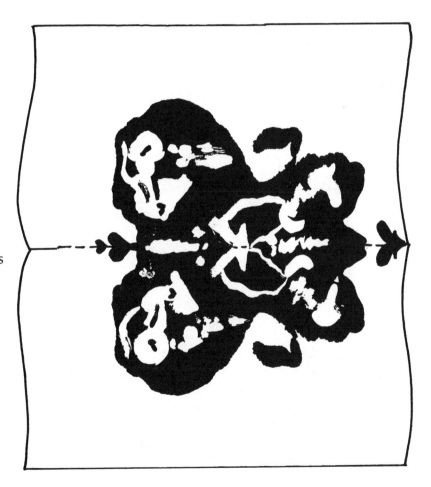

PUFF-IT PAINT

Thin paint can be transformed into designs when the artist blows into a straw and directs the paint into interesting patterns and fan-like designs. Blow gently to begin with, and then experiment with different strengths of blowing and tilting of the straw.

MATERIALS
Use any of the following for the paint in cups-
    food coloring mixed with water
    thin tempera paint
    watercolor paint
drinking straws
non-absorbent paper, such as fingerpainting paper
paintbrush or spoon, one for each color

PROCESS
1. Place the paper on the table.
2. Spoon or brush a little paint or food coloring on the paper.
3. Point a straw in the direction the paint will go and place the straw to the lips. Blow. The paint will spread out like a fan and make patterns and designs.
4. Continue blowing the paint until satisfied with the design.
5. Dry completely.

VARIATIONS
- Blow the paint with a turkey baster instead of a straw. Use larger paper.
- With adult supervision, use black ink instead of paint to make black and white designs.
- Sprinkle dry tempera paint on the paper. Blow clear water through the paint.
- Color with crayon on the paper first, and then add the paint. Blow with a straw and watch the crayon resist the paint.

PUFFY PAINT DOUGH

MATERIALS
equal parts of flour, salt, and water
liquid tempera paints
spoon and bowl for each color
cardboard squares, matte board, or heavy paper
empty plastic squeeze bottles such as –

ketchup	mustard	shampoo	frosting decorating tool

 Flour, water, salt, and paint combine to make a squeezable dough with the best qualities of both paint and dough. When the colors are squeezed on the paper they will not mix even when they pool together. The mixture then hardens in a puffy shape with a glistening quality from the salt.

PROCESS
1. Mix equal parts of flour, salt, and water in a bowl. Prepare several different bowls for as many colors as you wish to make.
2. Add liquid tempera paint for color in the desired amount to each bowl. For pastel colors, add a little paint. For bright colors, add more paint.
3. Pour the mixture into the empty squeeze bottles. The bottles with wider openings are the easiest to fill.
4. Squeeze the mixture onto the base paper, making designs or drawings. Experiment with different colors touching each other.
5. Dry until hard and shiny.

HINT
• The mixture will store in a covered container in the refrigerator for about a day or two, but will eventually dry out. Washing out containers is much easier when the mixture is still fresh and moist.

CAR TRACKS

If there has ever been a reluctant artist, this activity will invite and involve even the most stubborn individual. Driving toy cars through paint and then across large sheets of paper is not only beautiful, it's great fun.

MATERIALS

liquid tempera paint
liquid starch
cookie sheet or tray with sides
paintbrush for mixing
small toys cars
other toys with wheels
large sheets of paper

PROCESS

1. Pour a puddle of liquid starch onto the cookie sheet or tray.
2. Squeeze a big spoonful of paint into the starch puddle.
3. Mix the paint and starch together with a paintbrush.
4. Roll a small toy car through the paint.
5. Then drive the car over a piece of paper creating designs and tracks. Place the car back on the tray.
6. Roll other wheeled toys through the paint and then over the paper.
7. Dry the painting completely.

VARIATIONS

- Place several different colors of paint on the tray so a mixing of colors will occur both on the tray and on the paper.
- Incline a board, cover the board with paper, and then place blobs of paint on the paper. Next roll cars or other objects through the paint, down the incline. Have paper at the bottom to catch drips and toys.
- Experiment with pressing the car's wheels onto an ink pad or food coloring on wet paper towels, and then drive the car over paper.
- Paint a "Car Tracks" play mat for toy cars to drive on when the sheet of paper is dry.

MARBLE ROLL

MATERIALS
Collect any of the following for the paint container –
- round cake pan
- shoe box
- baking pan
- plastic tray with sides

Collect any rolling objects for the painting tool –
- marbles
- ball
- hard-boiled egg
- ball bearings
- orange

tempera paints in cups
spoons for each cup
bowl of water
paper towels
paper or paper plates

Rolling a marble or other round object through paint creates engaging patterns that are delightful to make. The shape of the container can also contribute to the possibilities of design, so collect a variety of containers and round objects, and see what happens.

PROCESS
1. Cut paper to fit the pan or box. Hint: A paper plate fits nicely in a round cake pan.
2. Place a marble in each cup of paint.
3. Spoon several different marbles out of the paint and place on the paper in the pan or box.
4. Roll them around by tipping and tilting the pan. They will leave colored trails on the paper.
5. When the design is complete, remove the marbles with a spoon and plunk into the bowl of water to clean. Then remove them from the water and place back into the cups of paint to begin again.
6. Remove the paper from the box or pan and dry.

HINT
- If working with a large group of artists, have lots of marbles on hand.

VARIATIONS
- Put spoonfuls of paint on the paper in the pan and then place one marble in the pan. Tilt and turn the pan so the marble rolls through the puddles of paint, making designs as it rolls.
- The shape of the container will contribute to the type of design that occurs. Try round, square, large, and small containers.
- If rolling a hard-boiled egg through puddles of paint, the egg will become decorated, although quite messy.

FINGERPAINTING

Fingerpainting is a basic sensory experience that children love because they can feel the paint moving and sliding about on the paper and between their fingers. There are several recipes listed in Chapter 7 of this book, but two of the best are listed below. The first recipe is the easiest. The second is a cooked fingerpaint that is smooth and can be painted with while still warm.

MATERIALS
RECIPE 1 – Easy Starch Fingerpaint
   Mix liquid starch and tempera paint with the hands right on the fingerpaint paper.
RECIPE 2 – Warm Cornstarch Fingerpaint
   Boil 3 parts water in a pan and remove from the heat. Dissolve 1 part cornstarch in a little cold water. Add to the hot water, stirring constantly. Boil until clear and thick for about one minute. Add food coloring or paint.
smooth paper
masking tape, optional
apron
bucket of soapy water
newspaper-covered drying area

PROCESS
1.   Choose a fingerpainting recipe.
2.   Prepare the artist and the table for fingerpainting by covering each appropriately.
3.   Place the paint on the paper (which can be taped to a sheet of newspaper on the table).
4.   Draw with hands, fingers, fingernails and even arms and elbows through the paint on the paper. Other tools may be added to the fingerpainting such as sticks, toothpicks, cotton balls, and so on.
5.   When the painting is complete, the artist should immediately go to the bucket of soapy water and wash hands. Help may be needed removing the apron.
6.   Carry the fingerpainting on the newspaper to a drying area. Dry completely.

HINTS
•   Although messy, fingerpainting is the most basic art experience for children. Some children don't like to be messy and choose not to participate. This is normal.
•   If a flat fingerpainting is desired, the dry painting can be covered with a clean sheet of newspaper and pressed with an old iron set on medium, no steam.

VARIATIONS
•   Fingerpaint over paper that has first been colored brightly with crayon.
•   Fingerpaint with wallpaper paste, hand lotion, shaving cream, or chocolate pudding.
•   Add other ingredients to the fingerpaint recipes such as: scented oils, vanilla, sand, talcum powder, and so on.

PAPER DIP AND DYE

MATERIALS
food coloring, paper dye, or powdered vegetable dye
water
small bowls
coffee filters

PROCESS
1. Mix food coloring with water in small bowls. If using paper dye, only use 1/8 teaspoon or so in each bowl.
2. Next, fold coffee filters in any manner.
3. Dip the corners and edges into the dishes of color.
4. Unfold.
5. Dry.

HINTS
- Decrease drying time by placing the damp paper in a warm oven or in the microwave until paper is dry.
- Small containers of paper dye in powder form are available in art stores. They are far more brilliant in color and last much longer than food coloring. Mix up quart containers with dyed water so more color is always ready.

VARIATIONS
- Fold and dip paper towels, napkins, white wrapping tissue, or other absorbent paper into the colored water. Dry on newspaper or plain newsprint. Unfold carefully.
- Dyed sheets of white wrapping tissue make a nice gift when folded, stacked, and tied with a ribbon.
- Dyed white wrapping tissue can be used to wrap gifts. So can coffee filters or other papers.
- Coffee filters can be used for a display of flowers and butterflies.
- Wrap a pipe cleaner around the center of a bunched-up coffee filter to make a flower on a stem.
- Spread a coffee filter out on newsprint and dab color on it with a cotton swab, paintbrush, or eyedropper filled with colored water.

 Oohs and aahs consistently accompany the process of dipping absorbent paper into cups of bright colored dye. Fold coffee filters in any fashion or style, and dip a small section or corner into the dye. See the colors spread through the paper and create new colors. When the coffee filters dry, the resulting colors have changed even more and blended into new shades and hues.

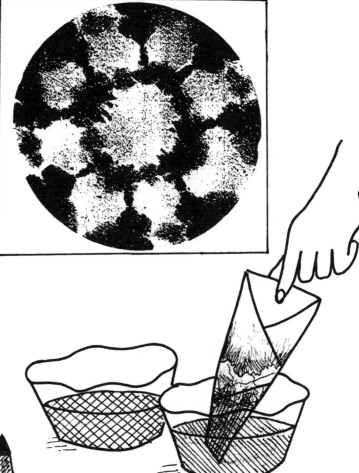

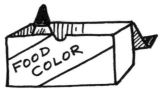

SPATTER PAINTING

 Artists often discover spattering paint on their own before it is a suggested art process. This version of spattering paint helps contain the spatters in a cut-away box supplied with window screen and toothbrush to create spatters everyone can enjoy. Although fairly involved preparation is required, the process of spattering paint is worth the effort.

MATERIALS
cardboard box large enough for the paper and frame
paper
tape
newsprint
window screen stapled to the back of an old picture frame
shapes or stencils cut from paper
items collected from nature, such as –
    leaves   flowers   weeds   ferns
toothbrush
tempera paint in cups

PROCESS
1. Cut away the top and one large side of the cardboard box to make a work area that will protect walls and floors.
2. Tape the paper to the center of the newsprint, and place in the cut-away cardboard box.
3. Place a stencil or an item from nature onto the paper that will become the pattern in the spatter painting.
4. Place the picture frame upside down on the paper.
5. Pick up a small amount of paint on the toothbrush.
6. Rub the toothbrush back and forth across the screen to make spatters on the paper.
7. When satisfied with the spatter painting, lift the screen and remove the shapes or nature items. A spatter painting stencil will be left.
8. Remove the paper to a drying area.
9. Rinse the screen and toothbrush under clear water in the sink when finished.

VARIATIONS
- Draw or paint with glue on paper. Place the screen over the glue design. Then rub colored chalk on the screen and the particles will stick to the glue on the paper beneath.
- Fill a container 1/3 full with cornstarch and water mixed very thin and liquid. Paint the paper with this mixture. Place a stencil or nature item on the paper. Place the screen over the paper. Rub the chalk on the screen and the powder will fall through and stick to the paper.
- Simply shake a brush filled with paint over paper. The shaken spatters, dots, blobs, and spots will create a painting. Use stencils too, if desired. Work outside.

POWDER PAINTING

MATERIALS
powdered tempera paints in small, flat pans or plates (one color for each pan)
paintbrushes
liquid starch in container
liquid starch in small bowl
jar of water for rinsing
paper

 Dabbing powdered tempera paint onto liquid starch is like mixing paint right on the brush. The powder dissolves and becomes thick paint, creating a texture unlike that created by normal painting techniques.

PROCESS
1. Pour a puddle of liquid starch from the starch container directly onto the paper.
2. Paint the starch over the paper with the paintbrush. Paint the entire paper, or paint designs.
3. Dip the paintbrush into the small bowl of liquid starch to moisten it.
4. Then dip the paintbrush into the pan of powdered tempera paint. Dab the paint powder onto the damp, starched paper, the starch and paint combining and becoming a thick paint. Use one color or many colors of paint. Rinse the paintbrushes as needed.
5. When the painting is finished, dry completely.

VARIATION
*   Sprinkle powdered tempera paint on paper, and then paint through it with a paintbrush filled with liquid starch, water, or thinned white glue.
*   Moisten a sheet of paper with water. Paint with powdered tempera paint directly on the moistened paper.
*   Moisten a sheet of paper with water and sprinkle tempera paint on the wet paper. When dry, draw designs on the painting with black permanent felt pen.

PALETTE PAINTING

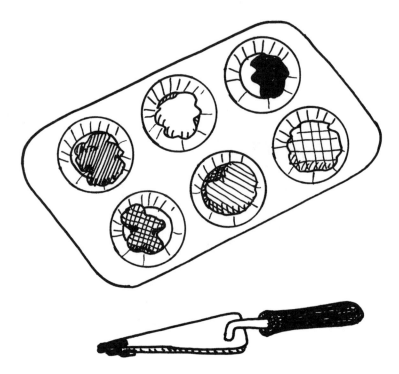

Painting with a palette knife allows the artist to see colors mix, to experiment with painting strokes and design, and to manipulate thick paint. First experiences often turn out to look something like mud, but further experiences will yield more pleasing results. All painting experiences are of value from the very first to the most advanced.

MATERIALS

thick fingerpaints in muffin tin or shallow cups
any of the following palette painting tools –

    palette knife   craft stick
    plastic knife   tongue depressor

cardboard, matte board, or heavy paper
easel or table

PROCESS

1. Decide to work at a table or an easel. If working at an easel, the artist will need to hold the muffin tin with paints in the non-drawing hand or set cups of paint in the easel tray.
2. Using a palette knife or similar tool, spread paint on the matte board surface in the same way that peanut butter is spread on bread or frosting on cake.
3. Push the paint about, making designs in the thick paint.
4. Add more paint colors and mix the colors right on the painting surface. Experiment with the end, sides, and point of the palette knife or tool.
5. Dry the painting overnight.

HINTS

- Remember that the process of palette painting is more important than the finished product. The experience of mixing and mooshing the paint on the paper will outweigh any artistic results.
- Allow for experimentation and have a large supply of paper or matte board on hand.

VARIATIONS

- Use additional tools for spreading, mixing, and painting such as a cotton swab, stick, spatula, spoon, or paintbrush handle.
- Place blobs of paint on a clean tray from frozen dinners. The artist stands at the easel and uses one brush to mix shades and tints of paint on the palette and then apply to the paper.
- Use a real artist's palette and a real palette knife.

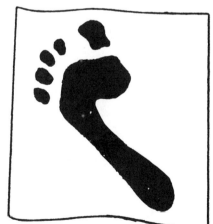

PRINTING
chapter 4

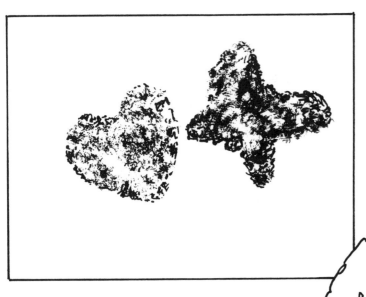

SPONGE PRINT

 Printing with a sponge is a basic art experience commonly seen as sponge painted leaves on a painted brown tree. Artists can create far more ideas than fall trees if given the materials to do so. Sponges can be cut in squares or cut with scissors into more complicated shapes. Dab the sponge into tempera paints of any color and then dab onto paper. The design is up to the artist. Fall trees? Possibly, but expect to see more variety of individual exploration and expression.

MATERIALS

sponges cut in squares or other shapes
pinch style clothespins
tempera paints
pad of wet paper towels on a grocery tray
newspaper
scissors
paper

PROCESS

1. Cut sponges into squares or other designs.
2. Pinch the sponge with the clothespin as a handle for painting with the sponges.
3. Dab the sponge into the paint on the grocery tray.
4. Then dab the sponge onto the paper making a sponge print. Several prints can be made before re-dabbing the sponge.

VARIATIONS

- Create patterns for wrapping paper, such as a heart, 2 squares, a heart, 2 squares, and so on.
- Sponge print on other materials such as fabric, wood, rocks, book covers, placemats, book marks, and so on.
- Sketch a pencil line design and print on the design.
- Use sponge printing for the texture on a large mural for the grass, fields, sky, or sea.
- Sponge print a wall or concrete floor with latex enamel paint for a permanent design. Practice on paper first.
- Paint with a sponge like a paintbrush instead of making prints.

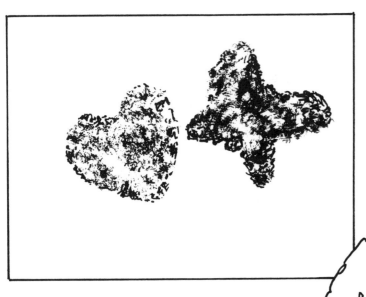

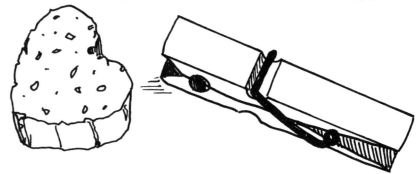

VEGGIE PRINT

MATERIALS
cutting and digging tools, such as –

| knife | nail | pencil | scissors | apple corer |

Choose a fruit, vegetable, or food from what is on hand in the refrigerator or cupboard –

| potato | celery | cauliflower | carrot | lettuce head |
| apple | citrus | parsnip | jicama | leek |

tempera paints mixed with liquid starch on flat dishes
paintbrushes
newspaper to cover table
paper, different colors and varieties
paper towels
tape

PROCESS
1. Cover the table and mix the paint. Place the plates of paint on the table, taping them down to prevent spills.
2. Choose a vegetable that can be cut into shapes or have designs cut into it such as a potato or a carrot.
3. Experiment with making prints by pressing the cut design into the paint and then onto the paper. Another approach is to paint the food with a paintbrush and then make a print.
4. Next, choose a food that can be cut in half to reveal a natural pattern within, such as an apple, artichoke, grapefruit, or cauliflower. Repeat the printing process.
5. Foods will no longer be edible, although it is possible to cut away the painted parts and rinse the remainder until very clean. I prefer to appreciate the food for its artistic use. However, if food coloring is used instead of paint, there is no reason why the food cannot be cleaned and eaten. Pink celery should still taste just fine!

VARIATIONS
• Create a flower garden mural with cabbage-half blossoms, lettuce head blooms, and other flowers and grasses made from Veggie Prints.
• Work on absorbent paper and use vegetable food dye for a different look to the print.
• Use inks instead of paint. Do not eat inked vegetables.

 A potato has always been one of the most versatile and inexpensive printing tools available because it can be cut into shapes that make creative art and design when dipped into paint and then onto paper. Why not take a look at the abundance of shape and design found in other foods, such as: the heart of celery makes a rose print, the interior of an artichoke makes a flower print, corn on the cob makes a bumpy trail. There are more designs to be discovered in other vegetables, fruit, and gadgets, too.

 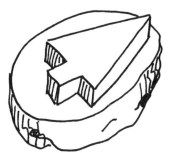

JUNK PAINTING

Mix some bright colors of tempera paint. Then dip junk collected from around the house, classroom, garage, or trash, that look like they may have interesting shapes when printed on paper. The paint makes a thick, bold print that when overlapping other prints, makes new colors and interesting new shapes and designs.

MATERIALS
Save throw-aways and junk materials to use for printing –

ABC blocks	feathers	rubber stamps
bolts	hands	screws
burrs	jewelry	shells
checker	keys	spool
chain	macaroni	sponge
coins	nails	straws
collage items	nuts	toy pieces
cookie cutter	plastic pieces	washers
corks	pine cones	wire
cups	pipecleaners	...more

tempera, food coloring, or watercolors in styrofoam tray
paper
newspaper

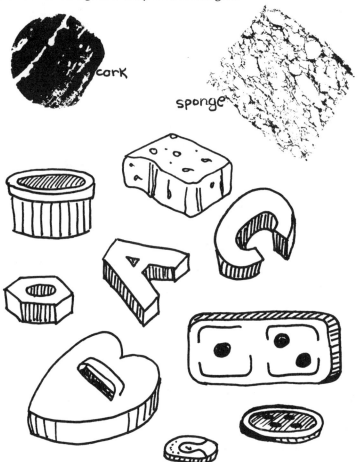

PROCESS
1. Cover a table with newspaper and place the tray filled with a thin layer of paint on the table. Tape it to the newspaper so it is less likely to spill.
2. Dip any piece of junk or interesting items into the paint. Or, use a paintbrush to brush paint on the part of the junk a print will be made from.
3. Press the junk onto the paper. Make lots of prints and then re-paint the junk piece or find a new piece to try.
4. Experiment with designs, patterns, or scenes.
5. Dry printed paper completely.
6. Rinse and dry junk. Keep the junk pieces in a bin for future junk printings.

VARIATIONS
- Create wrapping paper, banners, wallpaper, or greeting cards.
- See suggestions for Ink Pad Print, p. 85.

INK PAD PRINT

MATERIALS
ink pads (come in solids and multi-colors)
paper
newspaper
junk and gadgets small enough to press on an ink pad
collage items

PROCESS
1. Spread a pad of newspaper on the table for the printing work area. The pad will soften the workspace and make the prints more clear and detailed.
2. Collect junk and gadgets which can be used for inking prints on paper. These pieces will not be washed or returned to their former uses.
3. Place a sheet of paper on the newspaper pad.
4. Press a piece of junk, such as a lid from a jelly jar, onto the pad of ink and then press it onto the sheet of paper. One inking should provide more than one print.

HINTS
- The design and fun of the prints made will depend on what junk and gadgets are collected. Artists are often completely surprised that old worn toys or common kitchen utensils make shapes such as hearts, bumpy circles, or perfect stop signs. Help find some printing supplies by checking them out before hand. Then let the artists discover the surprise shapes, designs, and prints.
- Fingers and hands will get "inky". Soap and water helps, but the ink will just wear off in a few days. There are hand cleaners that will cut the ink, but they are harsh and just not really necessary.
- See suggestions for Junk Painting, p. 84.

JUNK PRINTING SUGGESTIONS
- Collect and save any of the following in a plastic tub –

any flat items	jar lid	roller for hair
clay ball	leaf	soft drink cap
coin	nail	stick
cookie cutter	old jewelry	toothbrush
eraser	paper clip	toy letters
finger(not in tub)	piece of wood	wire whisk
fork	plastic bag ties	what else?

Pressing "treasures" or junk onto an ink pad and then onto paper offers surprises in design and form as well as a new look at familiar objects and characteristics.
A toothbrush looks something like a caterpillar or a fuzzy flower. An old wire whisk resembles a target or concentric circle design. A plastic toy can have a surprising heart shape that wasn't readily visible. Discovery is a major part of printing with familiar objects.

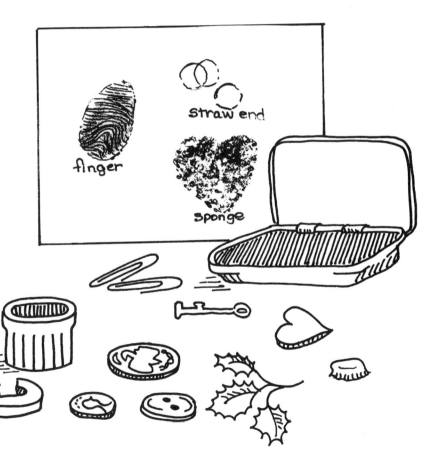

finger
straw end
sponge

FINGERPRINTS

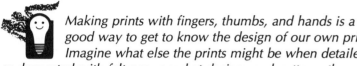

Making prints with fingers, thumbs, and hands is a good way to get to know the design of our own prints. Imagine what else the prints might be when detailed or decorated with felt pen, or what designs and patterns the prints can make.

MATERIALS
fingers
ink pad
paper
felt pens

PROCESS
1. Press a fingertip or thumb onto an ink pad. Ink pads come in solid colors and rainbow stripes.
2. Press the inked fingertip onto a piece of paper. Several prints should be possible before re-inking the fingertip.
3. Repeat as often as desired, making designs, patterns, or shapes. Use different fingers, thumb, and other parts of the hand.
4. Decorate the prints with felt pen for details, if desired.

HINT
- Hands can be washed in soap and water, but some ink will most likely be left on the skin. It will wear off in a few days.

VARIATIONS
- Color fingertips in other ways such as –
    with a felt pen
    in tempera paint on a pad of wet paper towels
    in food coloring on a wet pad of paper towels
    in watercolor paints
- Use felt pens to decorate the prints as flowers, bugs, birds, characters, pets, or other creatures or monsters.
- Create characters and design a storybook or picture with a story.
- Decorate greeting cards, note pads, or stationery. Photocopies of stationery can be made to reproduce a stack of matching paper for a gift or a set of greeting cards for the holidays or other celebrations.

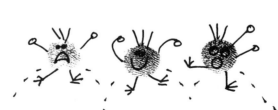

GLUE-ON PRINT

MATERIALS
materials to glue on a base for printing
base for gluing materials to
glue
scissors
ink pad or tempera paint on a pad of wet paper towels
paper to print on

Printing with "stuff" that has first been glued to a base for easier pressing, printing, and general handling is another basic art experience that has almost unlimited materials and possibilities in both creative combinations and in design. Experiment with materials and what types of prints they make.

SUGGESTIONS FOR –
MATERIALS TO GLUE ON A BASE
cardboard	sponge
heavy paper	string
innertube	styrofoam
leaf	tape
shoe insole	wood

BASES TO GLUE MATERIALS ON
brayer	frozen push-up-stick	rock
cardboard	paper plate	rolling pin
cardboard tube	pencil	styrofoam tray
craft stick	plaster	wood block

PROCESS
1. Choose a material and glue it on a chosen base. For example, glue a piece of a shoe insole which has been cut into a shape with scissors onto a block of wood.
2. When the glue has dried, hold the block and press the glued-on shape into a pad of paint and then onto a sheet of paper.
3. Make many repeat prints of the same shape, or make other combinations of printing materials and print on the same paper. (See illustrations for suggestions.)
4. Repeat as often as desired. Dry.
5. Rinse or wipe the inked or painted materials if desired.

HINTS
• Hands can become stained with paint or ink which will wash off somewhat, but not entirely. Color or stain will wear off in a few days.
• Protect clothing appropriately.

VARIATIONS
• Cut letters and spell things or write names.
• Make wrapping paper, greeting cards, murals, or posters of printed designs.

WOOD BLOCK PRINT

 There are natural patterns and designs in the grain of wood. A wood block print shows these clearly. Experiment with and compare the sides and ends.

block print

twist prints

MATERIALS
block of wood with raised grain
tempera paint
styrofoam grocery tray
paper towels
paintbrush
paper

PROCESS
1. Place a pad of damp paper towels in a styrofoam grocery tray to be used as the stamp pad.
2. Press the rough, raised side of the block of wood into the pad of paint. Paint can also be brushed onto the wood with a paintbrush.
3. Press the block of painted wood onto a piece of paper. Experiment with twisting or sliding the block.
4. Add other block prints or other colors to the print.
5. Dry the print.

HINT
• Placing a thick pad of newspaper on the table or work area helps the print show more detail.

VARIATIONS
• Use blocks of varying shapes and grains.
• Glue shapes to the block made from materials such as –
  innertubes   shoe insoles   cardboard   yarn
• Wrap rubber bands or string around the block, and print.
• Print on white wrapping tissue or butcher paper to make wrapping paper.
• Experiment with patterns and interconnected designs.

CLAY PRINT

MATERIALS
play clay, such as Plasticine
styrofoam grocery tray taped to the table
damp paper towels
tempera paints
paintbrush
tools for designing clay for printing, such as –
    pencil, nail, cookie cutter, knife, spoon, and so on

PROCESS
1. Gently push a ball of clay against a flat surface or table.
2. Press any tools or materials into the clay to make a cut-in design. Or, cut away clay to leave a raised design. (see illustrations for results)
3. Brush paint on the surface of the clay or press the clay into paint on damp paper towels in a shallow tray.
4. Then gently print on paper. Several prints should be possible from one paint covering.
5. Repeat with different colors and designs.
6. Dry.

VARIATIONS
- Shape the clay into letters or designs for printing.
- Use clay prints for wrapping paper, wallpaper, or banners.

Clay is one of the most versatile printing materials because it can be cut, pressed, imprinted, or shaped to be any kind of stamp imaginable. It is also easy to clean and prepare for other uses. One of the more interesting characteristics of clay printing is planning how to make the design that will be the print. The artist can either cut or press into the clay for a recessed design (most common for beginning artists), or cut away clay for a raised design (a more abstract, experienced approach).

By wrapping string around a block of wood, a simple print block with easy design construction is created in a few minutes. The creativity comes from the variety of ways a single block can be turned to create different designs.

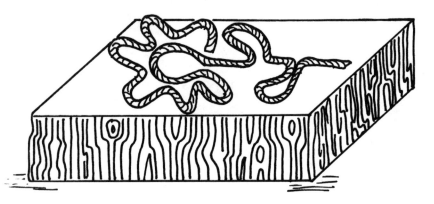

MATERIALS
string or yarn
blocks of wood
glue in a dish
tempera paint in shallow pan
paintbrushes
paper

PROCESS (Two techniques)
TECHNIQUE ONE –
1. Wrap string around a wooden block enough times to create a pattern of string. Don't cross string over itself or let it build up. Tie to hold.
2. Place paint in a shallow pan.
3. Press the block into the paint so the string soaks up paint. Or, paint the string with a paintbrush.
4. Make a print by pressing the block with string onto paper. Press more than once to make several prints. Then re-paint and print again.

TECHNIQUE TWO –
1. Dip string in the glue and arrange it on a block of wood.
2. Let dry.
3. Press the string design into a pan of paint and then onto paper. Make several prints.
4. Re-paint the design and print again if desired. Dry.

VARIATIONS
- Make wrapping paper by printing on butcher paper or white wrapping tissue.
- Create borders on a bulletin board.
- Press the block of string into an ink pad, food coloring, or other color medium instead of paint.
- Experiment with other materials that can be wrapped around a block of wood or glued to its surface for printing.

STRING ROLLER PRINT

MATERIALS
yarn or string
heavy cardboard tube, such as a mailing tube
paper
cushion of newspaper
tempera paints on large styrofoam tray or cookie sheet
paintbrush

PROCESS
1. Pour some paint in a styrofoam grocery tray or on a cookie sheet. To keep the paint moist, first dampen a pad of paper towels and place on the tray. Then pour paint on the wet towels.
2. Wind a length of yarn or string around a mailing tube or other cardboard tube. Cross the yarn over itself or in any way you like the yarn design to take shape.
3. Next, dab the string roller in the paint, turning or rolling it to cover the yarn all the way around.
4. Now, roll the tube across some paper and watch the design appear.
5. Re-paint the tube design and continue making roller prints.

VARIATIONS
- Yarn can be glued to a cardboard tube in any design. The yarn and glue must dry completely before making prints.
- Wrap string around a block of wood and make prints that do not roll.
- Wrap rubber bands around a tube or around a block of wood to make rubber band prints.
- Roll tape around a tube or dowel at an angle to make angle prints.
- Cut nicks and spaces in the edges of a wooden spool and roll it through paint, and then across paper.
- Glue shapes cut from the insole inserts in shoes or from tire innertubes to a rolling pin. Roll through paint and then across paper.

 Many different kinds of prints can be made by sticking things onto a cylinder or wrapping things around a tube. Choosing just a few examples to mention becomes a challenge. Any kind of roller printing is great fun and amazingly successful as well as surprising in the shapes and designs that appear. Experiment with other ideas and materials on a roller that might make great prints.

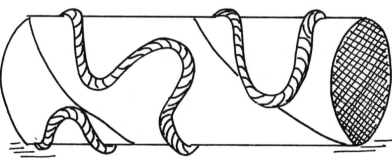

GLUE PRINT

Drawing with glue to make a design and then transferring that design to paper is like a simple printing press. The design works best if the glue lines are thickly squeezed from the glue bottle and then completely dried until hard.

MATERIALS
white glue in a squeeze bottle
heavy cardboard
thick tempera paint in a cup
paintbrush
spoon
paper
newspaper

PROCESS
1. Draw with white glue from a squeeze bottle directly onto the cardboard to create a design.
2. Dry the glue design overnight or until completely dry and clear.
3. Spread thick tempera paint over the dry glue design with a paintbrush.
4. Place a sheet of paper gently over the design.
5. Rub the back of the paper with a spoon to make the design transfer to the paper. Use moderate pressure with the spoon. Peek under the paper to see how the transfer is going.
6. Remove the paper, peeling from the corner.
7. Place the print on a sheet of newspaper to dry.
8. Dry completely.
9. Continue to make more prints if desired.

VARIATIONS
• Instead of a spoon, use gentle pressure of the hand to pat and rub the design through the paper.
• Experiment with different types of paper as well as with other tools for rubbing the design.

RELIEF PRINT

MATERIALS
cardboard or matte board
scissors
glue
tempera paint pad
paintbrush
rolling pin or brayer, optional
paper

 This Relief Print makes a solid, precise print from covering the cardboard shape with tempera paints and then pressing or roller-printing it on paper. Let different colors of paint overlap and mix on the paper.

PROCESS
1. Cut cardboard into a shape. Adult help may be needed because cardboard is hard to cut.
2. Glue the cardboard shape to another square or cardboard.
3. Dry completely.
4. Put some tempera paint on a pad of wet paper towels on a flat pan or a styrofoam grocery tray.
5. Press the cardboard relief stamp into the paint, or, brush the raised part of the stamp with paint.
6. Press the painted shape down on a piece of paper. Another technique is to roll over the back of the cardboard stamp with a rolling pin or brayer to ensure a more complete print.
7. Make as many prints as desired.
8. Let the printing dry.

VARIATIONS
- Cardboard shapes can be cut out and glued to a block of wood for an easy-to-hold printing tool.
- Make theme print designs for special days, such as –

holidays	pet day	spring	winter
harvest	sports	books	and more

MONOGRAPH

 A monograph is similar to fingerpainting on a flat surface and then pressing a paper on the fingerpainted design to leave a print on the paper. But in this art experience, a paper is placed lightly onto the paint and then a design is pressed into the paper. The design pushes a heavier layer of paint onto the paper and gives a different look to printing with paint.

MATERIALS
any smooth surface such as –
    table   sheet of Plexiglas   cookie sheet
tempera paint
liquid starch
dish for each color
paintbrushes
paper

PROCESS
1. With a paintbrush, cover a smooth surface such as a cookie sheet with a mixture of tempera paint and liquid starch. Several colors may be spread on the cookie sheet at one time.
2. Very gently place a piece of paper on the painted cookie sheet. Do not press the paper into the paint.
3. Using the end of a paintbrush handle, use heavy pressure and draw on the paper.
4. Carefully peel the paper off of the paint on the cookie sheet.
5. The monograph design will be transferred to the paper.
6. Make additional prints from the same paint on the cookie sheet. Drying paint can be moistened with a spoonful of liquid starch.
7. Dry the design.

HINT
- Results vary with this process of printing, but remember to work towards experimenting and exploring the process rather than looking for perfect results.

VARIATION
- Draw a design in the paint on the cookie sheet with fingers, paintbrush, or other tools. Gently press a sheet of paper onto the design, and then lift the paper to see the design transferred to the paper.

FINGERPAINT MONOPRINT

MATERIALS
tempera paints and liquid starch
cookie sheet or other smooth surface
paper
newspaper
old towel
bucket of soapy water
old iron (optional)

Fingerpainting is a basic art experience, but in this format, the mess that can cause some people to avoid the activity altogether is reduced significantly. Monoprinting is also aesthetically and artistically pleasing. Another benefit is that several artists can use the same cookie sheet and paint with only a little additional liquid starch added to moisten and extend the paint.

PROCESS
1. Pour a puddle of liquid starch in the center of the cookie sheet.
2. Add a spoonful or two of powdered or liquid tempera paint. Add more than one color if you like.
3. The artist mixes the paint by hand on the cookie sheet and then spreads the paint to fill an area suitable for fingerpainting.
4. Fingerpaint on the cookie sheet. Try fingers, hands, and even elbows, creating designs and patterns and enjoying the feel and smell of fingerpaint.
5. When a design is ready, rinse hands in a soapy bucket of water. Dry hands on the old towel.
6. Then gently press a sheet of paper on top of the paint design, rubbing with very light hand pressure back and forth over the design.
7. Peel the paper from the fingerpainting design and see the design transferred to the paper. Make a second print, and sometimes even a third can be made from the same fingerpainting.
8. Place the painting on a sheet of newspaper to dry.
9. When dry, if the painting has curled, place the painting face side down on newspaper; cover the painting with a second sheet of newspaper, and then iron the painting until flat with a moderately warm, dry iron. Adult supervision for the ironing.
10. The next artist to use the cookie sheet will only need a little starch to freshen and moisten the paint.

VARIATION
• Fingerpaint on smooth paper the traditional way, p. 76.

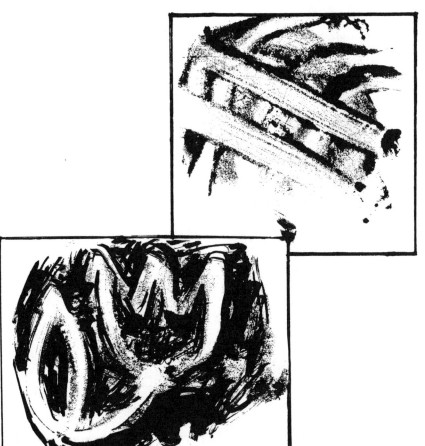

LEAF PRINT

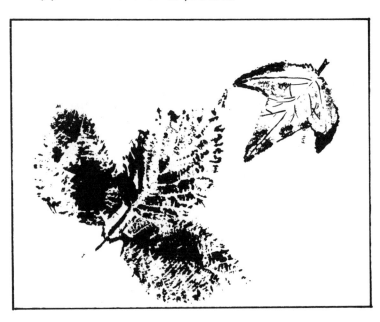

The natural beauty and variety of leaves can be captured on paper by first painting on the leaf and then pressing a soft sheet of paper onto the painted leaf. When the paper is removed, a leaf print will remain. Make as many prints from one leaf as you like.

MATERIALS
strong, fresh leaf
newspaper
paintbrush
bar of hand soap
jar of water
watercolor paints
soft paper, such as the paper towels used in schools

PROCESS
1. Place the leaf on a sheet of newspaper.
2. Rub the paintbrush on a wet bar of soap to help watercolor paint stick to the leaf.
3. Make a thick layer of paint on the leaf by blending watercolors together.
4. Cover the painted leaf with a piece of soft paper.
5. Rub fingers gently on the paper to transfer the paint to the paper.
6. Remove the paper to see the leaf print. Dry.
7. Repeat as many times as desired.

VARIATIONS
- Paint with tempera paints on a leaf. Make a print.
- Fingerpaint on a leaf. Make a print.
- For a rainbow effect, dab colored inks on a leaf with a sponge and make a print.
- Press a piece of fabric on the leaf for a print. Try using fabric paints for fabric leaf prints.
- Place a thick leaf on a warming tray and color on it with crayon. Then press a piece of paper on the leaf to transfer the warm crayon print to paper.
- Make a leaf stencil by placing a leaf on paper and then dabbing ink or paint on the leaf, spreading onto the paper. Remove the leaf and a stencil design is left. Do the same with paint on a brush, brushing from the leaf out onto the paper for a painted brush leaf design.
- Use other flat objects instead of leaves.

FISH PRINT

MATERIALS
dead fresh fish (flat, with large scales)
newspaper
paper towels
tempera paint
paintbrush
absorbent paper or white cotton fabric

 The reactions of painting on a fresh dead fish and then making a print from it range from squeals of disbelief to serious scientific and medical concentration. Whichever the reaction, the prints are very life-like. When the project is complete, thoroughly wash the fish and then cook for a delicious meal to share with the artist.

PROCESS
1. Place the fish on the newspaper.
2. Pat the fish dry with paper towels if wet.
3. Paint one side of the fish with tempera paints. Use one color, or multi-colors.
4. Place absorbent paper carefully on the fish. Then, with a dry hand, hold the paper in place and press it onto the fish.
5. Lift the paper off and place in a drying area. Several prints may be taken from one painting of the fish. When the prints are fading, re-paint the fish for more prints.
6. Thoroughly wash the fish in clear water in the sink. Find a tasty fish recipe and cook the fish to eat.

VARIATIONS
- Make colored prints of other sea life such as prawns, crab, small fish, and shells.
- Create a sea life aquarium mural with cutouts of all the sea prints assembled.
- Create fish or sea life prints using white cotton fabric. Experiment with fabric dye painted on the fish, instead of paint. Do not eat fish in this case.

BUBBLE PRINT

Printing with colored bubbles is a pleasant, happy art experience. Some people say that if you snip a little hole in the straw near the blowing or mouth end, the artists cannot suck in the bubble mixture, only blow out. Most artists only make this mistake once. If you are very concerned, wait until the artist is at least four.

MATERIALS
dishwashing liquid
tempera paint or vegetable dye powder
containers from yogurt or cottage cheese
paintbrush for stirring
straws
paper

PROCESS
1. Pour about 1/4 cup dishwashing liquid into a container. Make more than one container for different colors or multiple numbers of artists.
2. Next add paint to the dishwashing liquid until the color is bright. Stir gently with a straw or paintbrush.
3. Place one end of the straw in the container and the other end in the mouth. Blow on the straw. Do not suck in. The bubbles should billow and slightly flow over the edge of the container.
4. Apply the sheet of paper in a rolling motion over the bubbles for the most bubbly looking prints. Try not to press down flat on the bubbles although this still works.
5. Repeat the bubble print process for bubbles of several colors on one paper.
6. Dry.

VARIATIONS
- Powdered vegetable dye should be mixed with a little water and then added to the paint. These prints are more transparent and glossy than prints from the paint mixture.
- Cut out the bubbles shapes and glue to other paper.
- Experiment with bubble prints on paper such as white wrapping tissue or matte board.

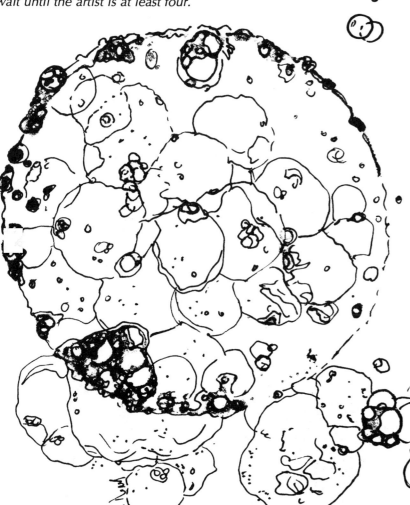

FEETPRINTS

MATERIALS
tempera paints mixed with liquid starch or water
large baking sheets or pans
long piece of wide butcher paper
towels
tub of soapy water
rocks to hold paper in wind, or tape to hold it to the floor

PROCESS
1. Cover several baking pans with about a 1/4" layer of paint.
2. Roll out the paper across the grass or floor. Use rocks or tape to hold the paper in place. Place the paint-filled baking pans at the start of the paper. Place the tubs of soapy water at the other end of the paper.
3. Stand in the baking pan of paint, and then walk across the paper. At the other end, step into the tub and rinse feet. Dry with the towel.
4. Change colors on the feet and go off down the paper again.
5. Experiment with unusual ways to walk to add creativity to the footprints.

HINTS
- Sometimes feet are somewhat stained by the paint, but the color will come off in a few days. Go swimming, wading, or play in the wet grass without shoes and the color will disappear even faster.
- The paper can become slippery, so change to a new piece if the paper is too full of prints. It can help to hold the hand of someone else while making prints.

VARIATIONS
- Dance gently and carefully.
- Make hand prints.
- Make prints with other parts of the body.
- Make prints with rubber boots, shoes, and footwear with interesting patterns.
- Try to guess which artist, which shoe, or which foot made which print. Kids are very good at guessing because they seem to notice details that adults often miss.

 Printing with paint on paper always requires an object that the print is made from. Look no further than your own bare feet for this activity! A warm day would allow working outdoors where the mess is less, but a hallway or roomy kitchen will do. Be prepared for squeals and cases of the sillies, and also have a soapy plastic tub handy for rinsing pretty-colored footsies.

dog

people

EASY SUN PRINT

For a crisp, sharp image caused by the sun fading colored paper, it is very important that the objects on the paper do not move. The day must be very sunny, bright and hot with no wind, rain, or other disturbances. This is the easiest sun print possible. However, the faded paper print will not last other than a few days.

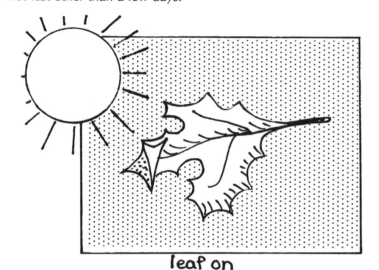

leaf on

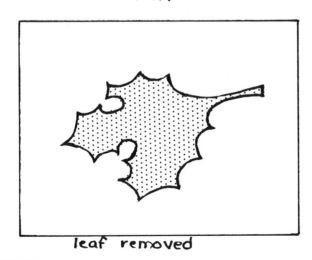

leaf removed

MATERIALS
one of the following bright papers –
    construction paper, bright colored poster board, or
    colored butcher paper
materials collected from nature
sunny day, very bright and dry
rocks or stones for weights
tape or glue

PROCESS
1. Go for a walk on a very bright sunny day. Collect items with nice shapes from nature.
2. Place a sheet of construction paper in the shade near the sunny area and lay out some of the nature materials on the paper. Work quickly so the sun does not fade the paper.
3. To keep the materials in place, use tiny pieces of tape or little drops of glue, but not enough to interfere with the design and print.
4. Carry the paper to the sun and place on the ground out of the wind. Place rocks or stones on the corners of the paper to hold.
5. Leave untouched until the sun sets. Bring the paper and nature items inside. Remove the pieces on the paper and observe the sun print.

VARIATIONS
- Buy a sun print kit at a nature or school supply store and follow the directions. Much like a blueprint.
- Use other objects for sun prints such as –

    scissors   hammer   cut paper shapes
    stencils   toys   pressed flowers
    jar lids   wooden blocks   bricks, rocks

- Make grass patterns by leaving objects on the lawn and fading the grass beneath. Water to restore the green grass after removing the patterns.
- Tape or pin objects to a bulletin board covered with bright butcher paper which is also in the sun most of each day. After several days, remove the objects and see the sun print left underneath.
- Create arrangements of nature materials on the paper, or use only one piece of nature to highlight.

PAPER DYE PRINT

MATERIALS
3 plastic quart containers filled with water
powdered vegetable dye or paper dye –
    three colors such as magenta, yellow, and blue
    1/8 teaspoon for each quart container
3 cups, 3 eyedroppers, 3 paintbrushes
newspaper
blotting paper (ink blotter) or other thick, absorbent paper
coffee filters

absorbent
paper

 Although the art technique of this project is similar to Paper Dip and Dye, p. 77, the focus is not to create colorful designs on the coffee filters, but rather, to create a print of the coffee filter on the paper underneath. The artist is encouraged to apply liberal amounts of color either from a brush or from an eyedropper, causing the blotting paper to absorb the design.

PROCESS
1. Spread a table with newspaper to protect table and absorb spills.
2. Drop 1/8 teaspoon of dye in each container of water. Shake the closed container to dissolve the dye.
3. Fill each cup with one color.
4. Place an open coffee filter on a sheet of blotting paper.
5. Using a paintbrush, create a colorful design on the coffee filter. Dye can be brushed, dribbled, dropped, or slowly soaked. Use an eyedropper in the same fashion, squeezing drops of color onto the filter. Use plenty of colorful liquid, letting it soak through to the blotting paper underneath the coffee filter.
6. When satisfied with the design on the coffee filter, lift it carefully and place it on another sheet of newspaper to dry, a secondary art experience to the print.
7. A print of the coffee filter will be left on the blotting paper.
8. Continue creating more coffee filter designs and adding to the prints on the blotting paper. The blotting paper dye print is complete when satisfied with the design. Dry.

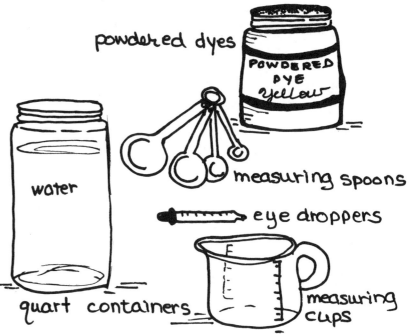

powdered dyes

POWDERED
DYE
yellow

water

measuring spoons

eye droppers

quart containers

measuring cups

HINT
• Artists' hands become colorfully stained during this art experience. Color will wash out somewhat, but staining may last for several days. Artists can wear latex doctor or painter's gloves for protection and for fun.

VARIATIONS
• See Paper Dip and Dye, p. 77, for other suggestions.
• Experiment with papers and color intensity.

paint brushes

coffee filters

CAUTION

MARBLING

Intense and brilliant colors can be marbled on paper by mixing powdered tempera paint, cooking oil, and mineral turpentine. When working with turpentine, children must be closely supervised. The colors and designs of the prints will be incredibly striking. Just like a snowflake, there are no two marbling experiences alike.

COOKING OIL
TEMPERA PAINT POWDER
MINERAL TURPENTINE

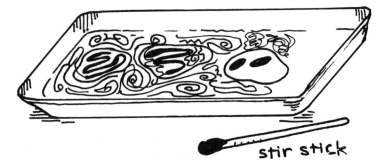

stir stick

MATERIALS
Powder Paint Mixture (see recipe below)-
   powdered tempera paint
   cooking oil
   mineral turpentine
disposable container for paint mixture
large styrofoam grocery trays taped to table
newspaper
plastic spoons
stir stick for swirling colors
white blotting paper or other paper
aprons or big shirts for artist protection
newspaper-covered table

PROCESS
POWDER PAINT MIXTURE: Use with adult supervison only.
   Mix 2 tablespoons powdered tempera paint in a disposable container with 2 tablespoons of cooking oil and 1 tablespoon turpentine. Make several colors.
1. Fill the tray half-way with cooking oil.
2. Drop small blops of the powder paint mixture onto the cooking oil.
3. Swirl the mixture on the oil very slowly and gently so the colors will float, swirl, and move in patterns.
4. Place a piece of paper on top of the floating colors and let it float for 20 or 30 seconds.
5. Then lift the paper off, turn it face-up, and immediately hold it flat so colors will not run.
6. Dry on a newspaper surface for several days.

VARIATIONS
- Marbling thin absorbent paper looks bright and transparent when taped in a sunny window.
- Fill an old bucket with water. Dribble three or four colors of enamel paint on the water's surface. Swirl with a stick or straw. Then dip a piece of matte board into the paint water, thin side straight in, and straight out again. The flat surfaces will be coated with swirled paint colors. Dry on a wire with clothespin for several days.
- Fill a shallow pan with water. Drip waterproof ink in various colors on the water. Then float a piece of paper on the water and ink. Lift the paper, and carry it flat to a drying area.

SCULPTURE AND MODELING

chapter 5

WOOD SCRAP SCULPTURE

Wood scraps are treasures with their beauty, originality, textures and aromas. Scraps from a custom picture frame shop are varied and unique. Some of the pieces have gold florentine design, others have fabrics embedded in the frame, and still others have carvings and moulding treatment that make them little works of art. Artists also enjoy the strange shaped pieces that come from a high school woodshop class, especially if the class is using a jigsaw and making curves and squiggles. Glue them together on a base, and the sculpture is complete.

MATERIALS
Collect an assortment of wood scraps such as –
   construction site wood
   picture frame scraps
   shop class scraps
   lumber yard pieces
white glue
any of the following -
   tempera paint
   crayons
   felt pens
masking tape
glue gun, optional with supervision
collage items, optional

PROCESS
1. Choose a piece of wood for the base, such as a square of plywood.
2. Select scrap pieces of wood and begin building a sculpture on the base wood.
3. Glue pieces together with white glue. If the glue won't hold, use masking tape to help until the glue dries. Then remove the tape.
4. When satisfied with the sculpture and sculpture is completely dry, the pieces may be painted, colored, or decorated with collage items, crayons, pens, or paint.

HINT
*   If one-on-one supervision is possible, a glue gun may be used with adult help. Glue guns have the advantage of rapid and thorough sticking and drying. However, they are also very hot and can burn anyone.

VARIATIONS
*   Build the entire sculpture and then go back and glue the pieces together.
*   Individuals can each make one sculpture on a heavy mat, which can then be joined and assembled with other single sculptures as one large display sculpture.
*   Add other collage items to the sculpture such as colorful yarns, ribbons, magazine pictures, sewing scraps, feathers, glitter, confetti, and so on.
*   Matte board and cardboard make excellent bases.

STICK AND STRAW BUILD

MATERIALS
coffee stir sticks
drinking straws
coffee straws
wooden ice cream spoons
tongue depressors
craft sticks
popsicle sticks
masking tape
other tape, optional

 Building with sticks and straws has infinite possibilities for the artist who likes a sculpture that grows quickly and stands on its own. Save drinking straws, coffee stir sticks, box juice straws, and other craft sticks to join together with masking tape for a variety of imaginative creations.

PROCESS
1. Join sticks and straws together with masking tape. Sometimes it helps to tear a quantity of pieces of tape before beginning and stick them to the edge of the table so that the sculpture can be created more quickly.
2. When satisfied with the sculpture, the work is complete.

HINTS
- A stick and straw sculpture can stand alone or can be taped to a base such as a styrofoam grocery tray, block of wood, or piece of cardboard.
- Some artists like to make intricate polyhedrons or engineering extravaganzas, while other artists make random shapes or spaceships. Imagination is the key.
- Straws can be shaped, cut, and bent and do not have to stay straight.

VARIATIONS
- Instead of using tape, pinch the end of the drinking straw and slip it into the end of another straw. They will join and make a strong sculpture.
- Use flexible "hospital straws" which bend at one end.
- To add the features to an animal sculpture or artistic decorations to any type of sculpture, glue on collage items such as yarn, glitter, or pasta.

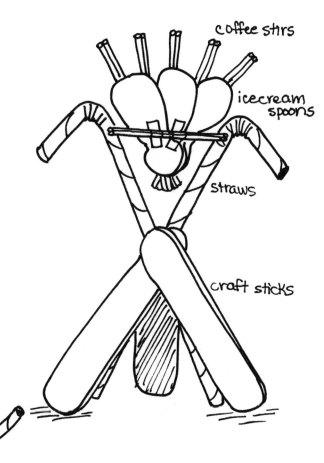

coffee stirs

icecream spoons

straws

craft sticks

coffee stirs

straw

NATURAL SCULPTURE

The best part of sculpting with natural materials is often going for a walk to find them, which heightens the imagination and gives flight to creativity. Assemble items and materials found in nature and glue them to a natural base for display. No paint or unnatural materials are necessary other than glue.

MATERIALS
natural materials such as –

bark	drift wood	gravel	seed pods
beach glass	dry flowers	nuts	seeds
bracket fungi	dry grass	pebbles	shells
burrs	dry weeds	pine cones	stones
cattail fluff	feathers	sand	twigs

white glue
glue gun, optional with adult supervision

PROCESS
1. Collect natural materials on a walk or over a period of time.
2. Arrange on a piece of base material such as driftwood or a shell.
3. Glue the pieces to the base. If pieces will not hold, use some masking tape to brace the pieces until the glue dries.
4. Dry overnight.

VARIATIONS
- Use a glue gun with complete adult supervision for a quick drying and sticking sculpture. Very hot. Extreme caution.
- Glue shells and glass to a flat rock for a beach theme.
- Cover a matte board or cardboard with burlap or felt and glue natural materials to the fabric.
- Glue nature items to other base materials such as –
    block of wood
    styrofoam tray
    cardboard
    picture frame
- Attach tiny dry flowers and grass to note cards or a picture that can be framed.

JUNK SCULPTURE

MATERIALS
Save materials to use for the junk in the sculpture –

beads	corks	nails	skewers
broom/straws	craft sticks	nuts	straws
burrs	dowels	pine cones	string
cattail fluff	embroidery floss	pipecleaners	thread
chains	feathers	plastic flowers	toothpicks
coffee stir sticks	jewelry	screws	wire
collage items	macaroni	sewing scraps	yarn

block of styrofoam such as stereos or TV's come packed in

 Part of the creativity of building a sculpture by sticking things into a block of styrofoam is saving and choosing the "junk" and imagining how it might be used. A simple piece of telephone wire can be curled and becomes a piece of art. Two nails held together by a strand of braided yarn are miniature imaginary telephone poles. In otherwords, Junk Sculpture is highly imaginative, and saving and collecting is part of the art.

PROCESS
1. Stick chosen junk materials into a block of styrofoam. Arrange, remove, rearrange, and create.
2. To further create, join materials together with thread and ribbon, or work wire around, interconnecting the sculpture materials.

VARIATIONS
- Weave fabric strips, ribbons, fibers, and other sewing scraps into the sculpture.
- Put the sculpture together and take apart many times.
- Build a theme sculpture such as –
    My Walk Collection
    Summer Litter
    Hardware Sculpture
    Junk Garden
    Things I Like
- Add drops of glue to the base of each item if the sculpture is to be saved, carried, or bumped.

WIRE SCULPTURE

 Who would ever think that the telephone cables from household phone system installation would be filled with an amazing variety of colored and striped wires that can be cut with children's scissors? The wire is versatile in that it can be curled, bent, woven, and created in almost any imaginable fashion. When the wire is poked into a block of styrofoam, the sculpture has a strong adaptable base and begins to take form immediately.

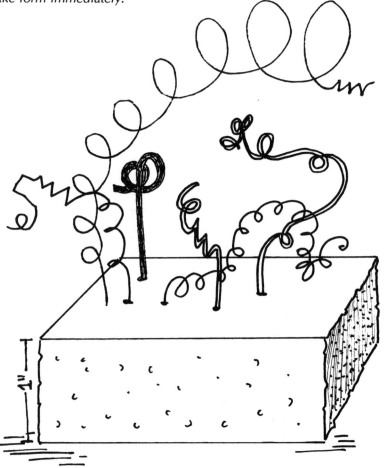

MATERIALS
insulated telephone cable, with colored wires inside
scissors
wire cutter, optional
styrofoam block
pencil
plastic darning needle or bamboo skewer

PROCESS
1. Remove the outer covering from the telephone cable to reveal the colored wires inside. Wires can then be cut with scissors, or an adult can cut wires with a wire cutter to prepare a large selection of wires.
2. Bend, twist, and shape wire. Experiment with coiling wire around a pencil, cylinder, or other shape.
3. Stick one end of the wire into a block of styrofoam. Feed the wire deep into the styrofoam to hold well. Sometimes it helps to push a plastic darning needle or bamboo skewer into the styrofoam to start a deep hole for the wire.
4. For a firm hold, push the wire all the way through a 1" piece of styrofoam and knot it on the back side of the styrofoam.
5. The sculpture is complete when satisfied with the design.

VARIATIONS
- Attach wire to nails or screws that have been hammered or screwed into a block of wood.
- Check with the telephone company for a large scrap of cable which has more colors than the more common phone installation wire.
- Add other junk, gadgets, or collage items to the wire sculpture such as –

| buttons | feathers | nuts | beads | hair rollers |
| keys | spools | colored pasta | paper scraps | jewelry |

- Create jewelry such as bracelets, rings, and necklaces.

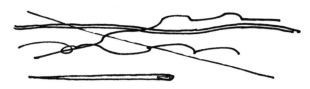

FOIL SCULPTURE

MATERIALS
aluminum foil
tape
straight pins (optional)
cardboard covered with foil for base (optional)

PROCESS
1. Crumple aluminum foil and shape into any form or sculpture.
2. If additional pieces of foil must be used, join multiple forms with tape or straight pins. The longest lasting sculptures are made with one large piece of foil.
3. Mount on a base if desired.

VARIATIONS
- Combine paper sculpture and crumpled foil for a Paper Foil Sculpture.
- Join many forms into one large foil sculpture display.
- Foil can be painted with tempera paint which has a few drops of dishwashing detergent added which helps the paint adhere to the foil.
- Create puppets on sticks.
- Create foil story characters, pets, or creatures from another planet.

 Crumpling foil and shaping it into a sculpture is easily controlled by artists. The foil can be painted when a sculpture is complete. Try to make one sculpture out of one large piece of foil instead of joining several small pieces of foil.

BOX SCULPTURE

Collecting an assortment of cardboard and boxes for a sculpture is almost as interesting as building the sculpture. Start assembling the boxes with tape, glue, or other materials and the sculpture grows and expands quickly before the eyes. Painting or decorating is optional.

MATERIALS
Collect an assortment of cardboard and boxes such as –

box lids	ice cream containers	paper cups
cardboard tubes	jewelry	pizza
copier paper	liquor case	shoe
egg cartons	milk cartons	stationary
hosiery	oatmeal	take-out food

white glue
any kind of tape such as –

masking tape	cellophane tape	duct tape

stapler
rubber bands
glue gun, optional (with adult supervision)
paint and brushes, optional
scissors

PROCESS
1. Collect an assortment of boxes and containers made of cardboard or paper.
2. Glue, tape, staple, and band boxes together in a sculpture letting the design of the artwork take shape as it grows.
3. When the sculpture is complete, paint and decorate if desired. Dry.

VARIATIONS
- Work on a box sculpture as a group.
- Cover the sculpture in papier-mâché and then paint.
- Build a box sculpture with other ideas such as –
    totem pole
    animal
    with only small containers
    that touches the ceiling
    with a door, walls, ceiling
- Add collage materials such as –
    yarn, string
    feathers
    ribbon, sewing scraps
    pom-poms
    and so on

TREE SCULPTURE

MATERIALS

tree branch without leaves, about 1 yard long
large coffee can filled with sand
paint
paintbrushes
collage and sculpture materials of choice such as –

ribbon	paper scraps	pipe cleaners
yarn	pine cones	colored wire
string	glitter	holiday ornaments, child-made
photographs	small boxes	anything

PROCESS

1. Find a tree branch without leaves, about 3 feet tall.
2. Place the branch in a large coffee can filled with sand to keep the tree branch upright.
3. Paint the branch, if desired. Dry completely.
4. Make decorations of any kind to hang from the tree branches. One popular idea is to make seasonal things such as Easter eggs or Halloween characters and hang them from the tree branch; change the decorations when the holiday or season ends.

VARIATIONS

- Make permanent hanging loops of pipe cleaners or wire so changes of decorations or ornaments can take place quickly and easily. The loops can be left on the branch at all times.
- Wrap and weave the branch with fabrics, ribbons, and yarns for a branch weaving. Other materials can also be added to the weaving such as dry grasses, paper strips, or leaves.
- Instead of stand, stabilize the branch by pouring plaster of Paris into the coffee can. Stick the branch into the plaster before it dries and hold in place until the plaster sets.
- Use a bucket instead of a coffee can.

 A tree sculpture is versatile in that the materials chosen to decorate the tree branch can be changed seasonally or can be created to go with a theme or special day. This sculpture can be an on-going, permanent art addition with changing decorations and creations to any classroom or home.

GARLANDS

 Artists can create imaginative garlands from almost anything lightweight that can be pierced and threaded with colorful yarn, and then draped about the room for special occasions or everyday enjoyment. Garlands also make festive necklaces or leis.

MATERIALS
Collect paper and lightweight materials such as –

art tissue cut in shapes	drinking straws, cut in short lengths
beads	packing peanuts
buttons	paper scraps
collage items	pastas with holes
crepe paper scraps	ribbon
cupcake liners	spools

masking tape, melted paraffin, white glue, or nail polish
plastic darning needle, optional
thread, yarn, embroidery floss, or string

PROCESS
1. Wrap a piece of tape around the end of the yarn or string to make a simple needle. Or, dunk the end of the yarn or string in white glue, melted paraffin, or clear nail polish. Let it set until hard. A third choice is to thread a plastic darning needle which has a large eye. Keep yarn or thread to a comfortable length, from 12 inches to 36 inches depending on the age or skill of the artist.
2. Any object with a hole in it or light enough to have a hole made in it is suitable for threading on a garland. Begin threading materials in a random fashion or with a planned pattern.
3. When one string is filled, tie a knot and then tie it to another string to make a longer garland. Many garlands can be joined to make one very long, colorful display.
4. Hang from the ceiling in a draping fashion, around the windows or doors, or around a special person.

VARIATIONS
- Follow a self-made pattern of threading such as: two yellow flowers, one bead, one straw, then repeat two yellow flowers, one bead, one straw, and so on.
- Create a Hawaiian lei with art tissue flower shapes and cupcake liners with straws to separate them. Use elastic cord for necklace or lei creations.
- Create a holiday garland for Christmas with red, green, gold, and silver decorations.
- Create a theme garland with materials that suggest such ideas as outer space, gardening, or litter.

MARSHMALLOW SCULPTURE

MATERIALS
toothpicks
mini-marshmallows, stale
baking pan
styrofoam grocery tray, optional base
piece of cardboard, optional base

 Assembling marshmallows with toothpicks is a favorite for artists, perhaps because some marshmallows never quite make it to the sculpture. The fruit-colored marshmallows are especially nice for this project and work best when stale and hard.

PROCESS
1. Spread mini-marshmallows in a large baking pan and leave exposed to the air for about two weeks or until they loose their powder-puff softness and feel hard to the touch.
2. Stick a marshmallow on one end of a toothpick. Then stick a marshmallow on the other end of the same pick.
3. Now add another toothpick, and continue building and attaching marshmallows and toothpicks in any shape or design. For a sculpture that stands on its own, build the sculpture with balance and symmetry.
4. Place the sculpture on one of the base materials if desired.

VARIATIONS
- Other materials for similar construction are –

dough balls	dried peas soaked in water overnight
corks	gum drops
bits of styrofoam	masking tape
large marshmallows	straws, skewers

- Join toothpicks with glue or tape and then paint.
- Cut out art tissue in a shape. Outline the shape with toothpicks glued to the tissue. Trim the extra tissue away. May be hung or taped in a window. Cellophane also works instead of art tissue.
- Sculptures can be painted, glittered, or drawn on with felt pens.

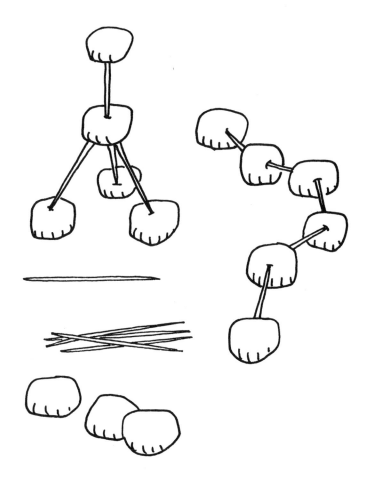

EDIBLE PARTY SCULPTURES

 Many foods lend themselves to artful arrangement. Designing with food makes it appeal to hungry artists and becomes part of a meal, snack, or party treat. The following sculpture suggestions are creative and tasty, and especially suitable for a party or holiday.

candy flower

marshmallow man

gum drop bugs

cookie-candy train

MATERIALS
Royal Icing ingredients –
    1-1/4 cups powdered sugar
    1 egg white, beaten until stiff
    1/2 teaspoon lemon juice
sculpture decorations –

cookies	crackers
raisins, currants	candies
marshmallows	M&M's
gum drops	nuts
candy sprinkles and pearls	lemon peel (can be cut with scissors)

bowl
knife
electric mixer
scissors
cardboard or heavy paper plate
aluminum foil

PROCESS
1. Make the icing by beating the egg white until stiff. Then add the sugar, beating well. When the icing is thick, stiff, and of spreading consistency, add the lemon juice. Beat well. The icing will be the "glue" of the sculpture.
2. Cover a piece of cardboard with foil; fold the foil around to the back of the cardboard as a base for the sculpture.
3. Using a knife or fingers, spread icing on the foil. Then begin sticking cookies and candy together to build a sweet sculpture. Some suggestions for sculptures are –

designs and shapes	playground or park
farm yard with animals and tractor	garden
animal in a pen	face
car with candy people	unusual creations!

    Use pipecleaners and other materials to add to the sculpture.
4. Dry for an hour or so.

HINTS
• Royal Icing dries out quickly, so keep the icing bowl covered with a damp towel. Icing stores in tightly covered containers in the refrigerator for about a week.

SNACK SCULPTURE

MATERIALS
Any of the following ideas make tasty, artistic snacks
when decorated and designed with imagination –

SNACK	DECORATE WITH
Cream of Wheat, cereals	fruit
toast with peanut butter	fruit
open-faced English muffin	pizza topping and veggies
peach or pear halves	cherries, raisins, berries
green salad	egg, olive, sprouts, tomato
macaroni and cheese	meats, veggies
baked potato	veggies, sour cream, cheese
mashed potato	shape, add veggies, gravy
dried fruits	raisins joined by toothpicks
cheese slices	cut or shape, fruits and veggies

PROCESS
1. Choose foods for a meal or snack based on what is available in the refrigerator or cupboard. Or go shopping and buy specific foods for the Snack Sculpture.
2. Wash hands. Set out ingredients.
3. Begin assembling or decorating the foods with other foods, garnishes, and decorative edibles.
4. Eat and enjoy!

VARIATIONS
• Create snacks decorated to highlight a season, holiday, special celebration, or to honor or surprise someone.
• Prepare a special decorated snack, wrap in a basket or box, and visit a friend in the hospital or nursing home with an artistic, tasty gift.

 Attractively arranging and decorating food can make it more appetizing and enjoyable. Adding fruit to cereal in a funny design or vegetables to salad to look like a clown should bring smiles to hungry faces.

cereal

bologna & cheese

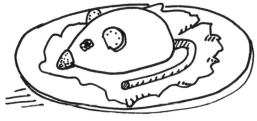

pear mouse

MOVING TISSUE SCULPTURE

When art tissue or cellophane is bonded to shapes like plastic milk carton rings or framed with toothpicks, the see-through shapes can be hung from the ceiling, a curtain rod over a window, crossed sticks, a coat hanger, or any number of other mobile structures. Because they are so lightweight, the bright and festive tissue mobiles stir and turn in the sunlight and from the slightest breeze.

MATERIALS
colored art tissue scraps
plastic milk bottle rings
white glue in a flat dish
scissors
thread

PROCESS
1. Dip one edge of a plastic ring from a milk bottle into the white glue in the dish.
2. Then stick it to a scrap of art tissue. Dry.
3. Dip other rings into the glue and then onto the colored tissue. Dry.
4. While the rings are drying, put a drop of glue on the edge of each ring. Place one end of a piece of thread into the glue so that the thread will dry in the glue.
5. When all the rings are dry, and when the thread ends are dry too, trim the extra art tissue from around the ring by tearing or with scissors. Be careful not to cut the threads.
6. Hang the see-through colorful circles from the ceiling, from a curtain rod above a window, on a Christmas tree, or anywhere you like.

VARIATIONS
- Cross two lightweight sticks and tie or tape them together where they cross. Tie some yarn to the crossed area for the main hanging loop. Then tie or tape the colorful circles from the crossed sticks so they can hang at different lengths and twist and turn in the light.
- Glue toothpicks to the tissue paper in triangle, square, or other shapes with their ends touching. The shapes should be "closed", or completely framed in toothpicks. When dry, trim the extra tissue away and hang these shapes as described above.
- Using liquid starch, stick art tissue scraps and shapes to wax paper or plastic wrap. Then stick rings, toothpicks, or other plastic shapes with "holes" in them to the paper or wrap. When dry, trim excess paper and hang from a coat hanger or other hanging idea.

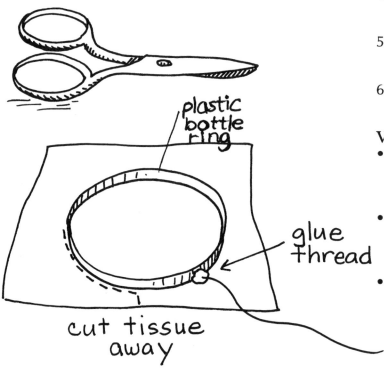

plastic
bottle
ring

glue
thread

cut tissue
away

PLAYDOUGH

MATERIALS

Mix and cook the following ingredients with a wooden spoon
in a saucepan on low heat until a ball forms –
- 1 cup flour
- 1 cup water
- 1 cup salt
- 1 tablespoon cream of tartar

Add coloring, optional, to the water before mixing –

food coloring	Or juice from cooked:
tempera paint	spinach
Jello	cranberries
Kool-aid	beets
crushed colored chalk	carrots

Some utensils to use with dough such as –

garlic press	plastic letters
cookie cutters	toys
knife	gadgets
rolling pin	fork
dowel	small hammer
jar lid	kitchen tools

PROCESS

1. Prepare the playdough.
2. Begin exploring the dough while it is still warm, if desired.
3. Roll, pound, stretch, pinch, pat, cut, twist, and explore the characteristics and possibilities of playdough.
4. When finished, replace the dough in a plastic container with a snap-on lid or a coffee can with a lid and store in the refrigerator or on the shelf.

VARIATION

- Whatever the artist imagines is part of the joy and versatility of playdough.
- Some days use only hands. Other days add tools and utensils.

Playdough is THE most basic and easy modeling experience for children of all ages and experience levels. There are many playdough recipes, some difficult and some easy, but the following is my personal favorite based on the attributes of smooth consistency and extended life. This playdough holds indentations and shapes, and doesn't stick to the hands as much as some other recipes. Keep in an airtight container in the refrigerator when not in use, although keeping it on the shelf works fine too. Allow for exploration and experimentation.

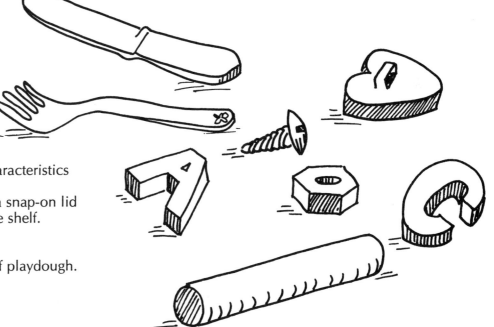

GOOP

Goop is not actually an art experience, but it is so strange, amazing, and thought provoking that it can't be left out of this sculpture chapter. When colorings are added and explored in the Goop, the mixing, blending, and swirling of the colors adds to the sensory experience of exploring such an unusual mixture.

MATERIALS
The mixture of Goop is 2 parts cornstarch to 1 part water. The following recipe is good for one or two artists to explore in a flat baking pan. Larger batches can be made up for a watertable, tub, or small plastic wading pool.
 1/2 cup cornstarch
 1/4 cup water
 measuring cup
 food coloring or thin tempera paint in cups
 tray, bowl, spoon, or pan

PROCESS
1. Mix cornstarch and water in a measuring cup.
2. Pour into a large, flat baking pan.
3. Explore and observe the Goop with bare hands. There is no finished product, just the process of exploring a strange mixture.
4. Add a few drops of food coloring or thin tempera paint to the mixture and mix in with the hands.
5. When finished, the mixture can be stored in an airtight container and reused.
6. Wash hands and clean up.

VARIATIONS
- Make an extra large batch in a tub for many hands to explore.
- Add more cornstarch and see what happens.
- Add more water and see what happens.
- Experiment with other colorings such as crushed chalk, crayon shavings, Jello, or powdered tempera.

BASIC BREAD CLAY

MATERIALS
Bread Clay Recipe –

Mix 4 cups flour and 1 cup salt in a bowl. Make a well in the center and pour in 1 cup warm water, mixing with the hands. Add 1/2 cup more warm water and continue mixing. Clay should not be crumbly or sticky, but should form a ball. Knead 5 minutes on a floured board until very smooth.

bowl
cookie sheet
board
plastic wrap
foil or wax paper

PROCESS
1. Prepare the dough from the above recipe in a bowl.
2. Work with a small portion of dough at a time and wrap the remainder of the dough in plastic and place in the refrigerator. Hint: If dough dries out, add a few drops of water and knead into the dough until smooth again.
3. Work on a sheet of foil or wax paper.
4. When a sculpture is complete, bake it at 325°F on a cookie sheet for 1 hour until hard. The dough should not give when tapped with a knife, but should sound hollow on both the top and the bottom.

VARIATIONS
- Some suggestions to make after basic exploration –

free-form objects	pretend foods for play –
beads	fruits
bugs, insects	vegetables
clay cranberries	meats
jewelry	cookies
molds, impressions	cake
napkin rings	breads
ornaments	pretzel
picture frame	baked goods

- For a colored dough, add food coloring or paint into the ball of dough and knead. Colored dough looks lighter when baked or dried.

Bread Clay is a modeling dough made from flour, salt, and water. It can be baked or air-dried, painted or colored, and is very manageable and an excellent modeling mixture. For a nice shine, coat the hardened art objects with white glue which has been thinned with water and brush on.

FLOUR AND WATER DOUGH

Flour and Water Dough is an uncooked play clay made from basic ingredients with nice results. The dough can be stored, but is best used the day it is made. Exploring with this basic dough needs no instructions - just play, explore, model, pound, and create.

MATERIALS
1 cup flour
1 cup water
food coloring or tempera paint for color
measuring cup, wooden spoon or hands, and a bowl
airtight container

PROCESS
1. Mix the flour, water, and coloring in a bowl. Mix with a wooden spoon or with bare hands.
2. When the dough holds together and is a nice modeling consistency, place it on the table.
3. Play, model, pound, roll, and explore the dough.
4. When finished, store the dough in an airtight container or discard.

VARIATION
- Like any playdough, other utensils and tools may be added to the exploration. See Playdough, p. 117, and Basic Bread Clay, p. 119, for suggestions.

SODA CORNSTARCH DOUGH

MATERIALS
1 cup baking soda
1/2 cup cornstarch
2/3 cup warm water
food coloring or tempera paint
saucepan
stove
spoon
board

 One of the unusual qualities that makes this recipe a good choice for modeling is that it is pure white and hardens quickly. It can easily be doubled, stores in an airtight container for several weeks, models very well and paints nicely too.

PROCESS
1. Prepare the dough:
   Mix 1 cup baking soda and 1/2 cup cornstarch in a saucepan. Add 2/3 cup warm water and stir until smooth. Cook over medium heat, boil and stir until like mashed potatoes.
2. Pour onto a board to cool. Then knead.
3. For color, knead coloring into the clay until blended, or paint finished sculptures with tempera, felt pens, or other colors.
4. Explore, model, and play with the dough. However, take note that the dough dries quickly.
5. Let dry until hard.
6. When dry, brush with white glue or clear nail polish for a shiny coat.

VARIATIONS
- Mix up several batches of different colored doughs and create holiday ornaments or decorations. For instance, twisting a red snake with a white snake will make a candy cane ornament. Or three white balls joined one on top of the other with other dough parts added could be a snowman.
- Make a set of storybook characters or puppets and stick them on bamboo skewers for a puppet show when they are dry. Attach yarn or other decorative materials to complete.

CORNSTARCH DOUGH

Cornstarch Dough is an especially nice cooked mixture because it uses so few ingredients and hardens relatively quickly. It can also be "speed dried" in the oven at 200°F for 1 hour. The texture is grainy and the appearance is pure white. Work with the dough while it is still warm from the stove for a tactile sensory experience.

MATERIALS
1/2 cup salt
1/2 hot water
1/4 cup cold water
1/2 cup cornstarch
saucepan and stove
wooden spoon
bowl
board
cookie sheet, optional

PROCESS
1. Prepare the dough as follows:
    Mix the salt and hot water in the pan. Boil.
    Stir cold water into the cornstarch in a bowl.
    Add the cornstarch-water to the boiling water and stir.
    Cook over low, stirring until like pie dough.
    Pour out of the pan onto a board.
2. When cool, knead until smooth.
3. Explore the dough freely, creating objects or sculptures if desired.
4. The dough will harden in one to two days or can be speed dried on a cookie sheet in an oven set at 200°F for 1 hour or so.

VARIATION
• See Soda Cornstarch Dough, p. 121, for suggestions.

SALT AND FLOUR BEADS

MATERIALS
1 cup salt
1 cup flour
1 T. alum
water
tempera paint or food coloring
toothpicks
thread, elastic cord, string, or leather thong

PROCESS
1. Prepare the bead clay by mixing 1 cup salt, 1 cup flour, and 1 tablespoon alum. Add enough water to make the consistency of dough. Knead and squeeze with the hands to make dough ready.
   Note: Tempera paint or food coloring can be added to the water or to the finished dough before kneading for color.
2. Pinch off a piece of dough and shape it into a bead.
3. With a toothpick, poke a hole through the bead.
4. To dry the bead, stick the toothpick and bead into a ball of dough.
5. Make as many beads in as many shapes and sizes as desired.
6. When the beads are drying, turn the bead on the toothpick once in awhile to prevent sticking.
7. When dry, string beads on an elastic cord, thread, string, or leather thong.

VARIATIONS
- Paint the dry beads with watercolor paint or felt pen. Coat the beads with shellac, clear acrylic, or some other fixative to prevent beads from staining skin or clothes. Thinned white glue works well. Dry.
- This dough is also good for making other shapes, sculptures, and ornaments.
- For a natural colored dough, add the cooking juice from vegetables such as, beets, spinach, carrots, and cranberries.

 Beads in all shapes and sizes – balls, cubes, animals, flowers, or tiny gems – make wonderful personalized necklaces or decorative garlands. The dough has a slight salt residue, so if the beads will be worn next to clothing or skin, they should be coated by an adult with shellac or clear acrylic.

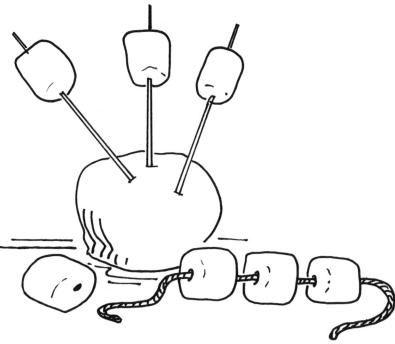

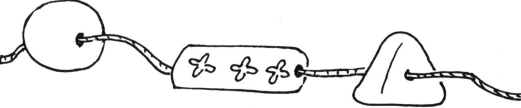

SAWDUST MODELING

 For an inexpensive mixture with impressive results, explore the possibilities of Sawdust Modeling. One of the best characteristics of this mixture is that when it is dry, it is incredibly hard and can be sanded with sandpaper before painting.

MATERIALS
This recipe is based on using about 2 parts sawdust and 1 part flour. Add water until stiff and squooshy:
    2 cups fine sawdust
    1 cup flour
    water (about 2 cups)
    food coloring or liquid tempera paints
    large bowl, wooden spoon
tempera paint and paintbrushes, optional
clear acrylic paint, optional
sandpaper

PROCESS
1. Mix the sawdust with the flour in a bowl. Slowly add some water and mix until squooshy and stiff.
2. Add food coloring or liquid tempera paint at this point if a colored sawdust mixture is needed. The mixture is actually a nice color in its "wood" form.
3. Mix and knead until the dough begins to take shape. Then play, model and explore the mixture and what it can do, how it feels, and how it smells.
4. Objects or sculptures will dry overnight, although large or thick objects will take longer. Dry in the sun if possible. Dries very hard.
5. When dry, objects can be sanded and painted, if you like.
6. Objects can be brushed or sprayed with clear acrylic paint for a clear shine, or brushed with thinned white glue.

VARIATIONS
- Sawdust Modeling works very well for a pottery look.
- Roll the mixture with a rolling pin, cut with cookie cutters, poke a hole, and when dry, add a ribbon or yarn for hanging.
- Great for simple Christmas tree ornaments.

CRAFT AND CONSTRUCTION
chapter 6

COLLAGE CONSTRUCTION

 An entire book could be written listing collage ideas! Collage offers infinite creative possibilities based on the materials on hand and the imagination of the artist. A list of collage materials is provided in Chapter 7 to motivate collecting and saving. As the artist experiences collage with new ideas, searching and collecting becomes part of the creative experience as the most ignored little pieces of trash become treasures for collage.

MATERIALS
Choose any collage materials from the list in Chapter 7, or find other materials. a base for the collage, such as –

styrofoam grocery tray	wood block
paper	paper plate
fabric	brick
cardboard	tile
matte board	shell
driftwood	wall

glue
glue gun, optional with adult supervision

PROCESS
1. Glue collage items on to the chosen base material.
2. Fill gaps and spaces. Use any design or style of placement.
3. Dry the collage completely.

HINT
• A glue gun allows for strong, immediate bonding of collage materials. However, extreme caution must be observed and one-on-one adult supervision is required.

VARIATIONS
• Use a theme for the collage such as –

seasons	a litter walk	happiness
emotions	my treasures	nutrition
fun, fun, fun	dreaming	colors

• A group collage can be created with everyone participating in gluing, constructing, and assembling on a large base surface such as a sheet of cardboard or plywood.

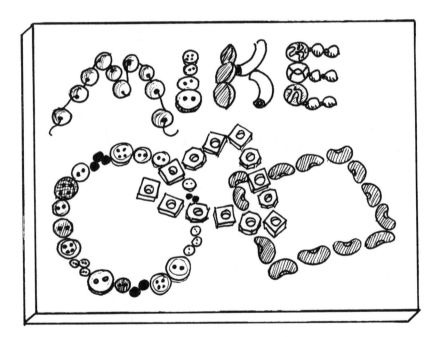

RANDOM WEAVING

MATERIALS
matte board
scissors
yarn
embroidery floss
tape

 The beginning experience of weaving is as simple as wrapping yarn through small cuts in cardboard and watching the shapes, colors, and interaction of the yarns evolve and unfold in pattern and design.

PROCESS
1. Start by cutting well-spaced slits in the sides of matte board squares. Make each slit about 1/2 inch long and about 1/2 - 1 inch apart, although there is no strict rule about the spacing. Cut either on all four sides, or on two sides only.
2. Pull one end of a piece of yarn through a slit so the end of the yarn is on the back of the matte board.
3. Tape the end of the yarn to the back of the board, if desired.
4. Begin wrapping the yarn from one slit to another, pulling the yarn tight through each slit. Yarn may crisscross, go front to back, or around and over, through, or here and there. In other words, wrap yarn in any way desired.
5. Add more yarn by starting in any slit, even one that has already been used, and pull the end into the slit snugly. Begin wrapping again.
6. Ends may be taped on the back of the matte board if desired.

HINT
• Adult help may be necessary with cutting matte board.

VARIATIONS
• Matte board may be cut in shapes other than squares, such as a circle, triangle, hexagon, diamond, heart, or oval. Odd shaped free-form shapes are interesting too. Shapes with holes cut in their centers or other imaginable possibilities are also effective.
• Use felt pens to color-in the areas between the yarn designs. Add stickers or other decoration if desired.
• Cover matte board with fabric or wrapping paper for added design.
• Make 1/2" cuts around the top edge of a cardboard oatmeal box.

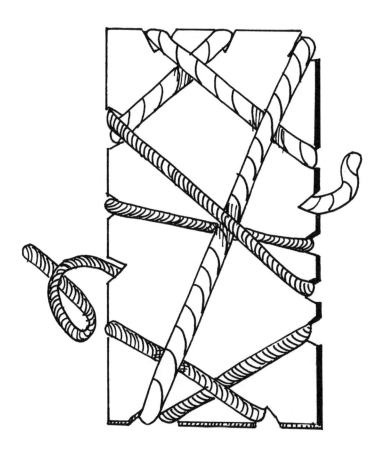

PAPER WEAVING

 Once an artist has experienced other weaving ideas, weaving on paper is the next step. A base paper is folded and cut as the "warp". Then strips of paper, the "woof", are woven through the base in any pattern or style. Much of the creativity of paper weaving depends on the variety of materials collected for the art experience.

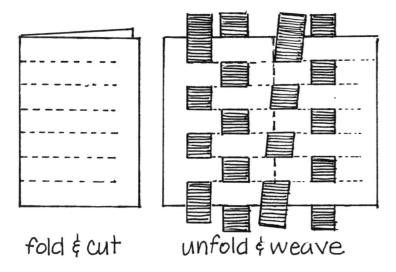

fold & cut   unfold & weave

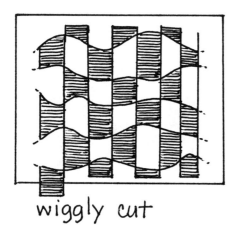

wiggly cut

MATERIALS

base paper –
    construction paper
    heavy paper, such as old file folders, tag board
    lightweight cardboard
    card stock
weaving strips, any width –
    construction paper
    card stock
    fabric strips
    twisted strips of newspaper
scissors, tape, glue, stapler

PROCESS

1. Fold a base paper in half.
2. Make cuts, straight or wiggly, from the fold to the open side, stopping short at least one inch from the edge.
3. Unfold.
4. Begin weaving a strip of paper through the base paper. Weave the strip over and under, or in any other style of weaving. Random weaving is often the choice of beginning weavers. More advanced weavers will discover other patterns.
5. Weave a second strip through the cuts of the base paper. Slide it next to the first strip for a tight weave.
6. Continue until the weaving is complete. Tape, staple, or glue the loose ends of the weaving strips to the base paper on the back of the base to hold.

HINTS

- Beginning weavers may use a random weaving style. More advanced weavers may weave a traditional over-under weaving style. For the over-under style, the first strip starts over, then the second strip will start under.
- Many other patterns besides over and under are possible.

VARIATIONS

- Weave on a paper plate.
- Use contrasting bright colors or materials such as strips of wallpaper or fabric.
- Laminate the weaving and use it for a placemat.
- Spread glue all over a piece of fabric and glue it to the base paper. Press out wrinkles. When dry, fold and cut the base. Then weave with fabric strips, paper, or other materials.

BASKET STITCHING

MATERIALS

any of the following baskets such as –
    flat picnic plate baskets
    loose weave cane baskets
    plastic berry baskets
    paper berry baskets
yarn or embroidery floss in many colors
plastic darning needle
scissors

 Stitching patterns with colored yarn through baskets is a good way to start learning stitchery and embroidery. The basket is a preformed base that is firm and is easier for young artists to hold while pushing the needle through the holes. A good beginning material for a younger artist is a plastic berry basket which is inexpensive or free and makes a smaller woven basket when complete. Older artists may prefer to stitch on a larger basket with more room for a complex design.

PROCESS

1. Thread a plastic darning needle with yarn cut to about 2-3 feet in length.
2. Choose a basket with a loose weave such as the flat baskets used for paper plates at picnics.
3. Stitch a pattern, random or planned, through the holes and spaces in the basket.
4. When one color or length of yarn runs out, tie it to the basket or tie it to a new piece of yarn and continue until the design is complete.

VARIATIONS

- Stitch through a loose weave burlap. Tape the edges of the burlap to prevent raveling. Or, ravel the edge but sew a line around the burlap to prevent raveling too far.
- Stitch through a mesh screen with large square holes (sometimes called hardware cloth) such as hamster cage lid material.
- Stitch through a grocery tray, punching holes as the needle progresses.

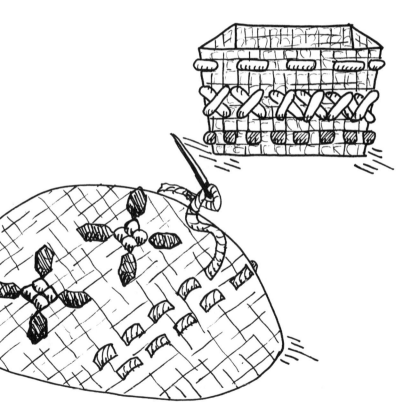

Weaving can be a complicated art experience if perfection is expected. Instead, allow for creative freedom in design and material, especially for younger artists who may not understand pattern and sequence yet. Experimenting and discovering what materials can do and how they go together in weaving will lead to more advanced weaving experiences in the future.

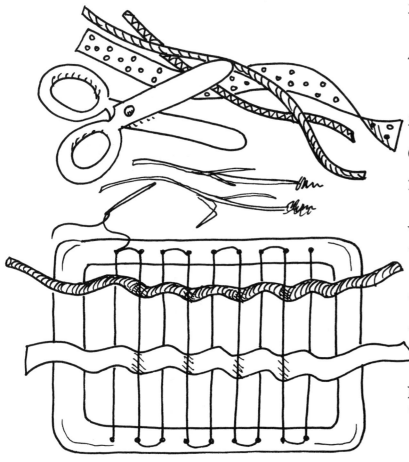

MATERIALS
styrofoam grocery tray
yarn threaded on a plastic darning needle
yarn, ribbon, wool, reeds, or grass for weaving
scissors

PROCESS
1. An adult can cut a square or rectangular shape from the center of the grocery tray. Save the piece for other art projects.
2. Thread a plastic darning needle with yarn and knot the end.
3. Push the threaded needle through the frame edge of the tray and pull it through. Then cross to the other side of the tray and push the needle and yarn through that side, pulling it through again.
4. Repeat the process back and forth across the cut-out area of the tray. These strands of yarn are called the warp. (The artist may have other ideas rather than stringing the warp simply back and forth, which is perfectly fine. Some very original ideas can be created.)
5. Weave ribbon, heavy yarn, or other materials through the warp, which is called the woof. Straight lines can be made, circles, or any shapes desired.
6. For an optional weaving idea, add long grasses, reeds, or other materials into the warp and woof.
7. When complete, tie the ends of the yarn or other materials on the back of the weaving. Some tape may also be needed.

VARIATIONS
- Weave other materials into the design such as –
  drinking straws   spools   pasta   washers   buttons
  paper with holes   pieces of styrofoam, cut and punched
- Use this weaving technique on a warp which has been built on nails hammered into two ends of a board.
- Several weavings joined together can form a large wall hanging.
  Cut slits in the top edge of an oatmeal box. Weave yarn through the slits, much like Random Weaving, p. 127.

HINTS
- Younger children usually need help or supervision with all the needle threading, knots that form, and cutting yarn, and so on.

BRANCH WEAVING

MATERIALS
branch with smaller branches growing out from it
heavy yarn, variety of colors
natural materials, such as –

grasses	feathers	corn husks	weeds
wool	shells	seed pods	flowers

weaving materials, such as –

fabric strips	newspaper strips	paper strips
ribbon	raffia	sewing scraps
strips of leather	leather thongs	embroidery floss

scissors

 Find a branch with smaller branches growing out of it and begin winding yarn from one small branch to the next. Other yarns, fabric, and natural materials like grasses, feathers, and weeds give the Branch Weaving an earthy look.

PROCESS
1. Cut yarn into 3 foot lengths.
2. Wrap yarn from one branch to another. Build a warp (the basic yarn strands that will be woven with other materials) from one branch to another.
3. When the yarn has been wrapped either as a warp or as a more random design, begin weaving grasses, wool, weeds, and other yarns and fabrics through the warp, or through the first wrapping of yarn. Thread through, over, and under.

HINTS
- Tie a knot or loop the yarn around the branch to start the wrapping.
- Some artists will prefer to weave in a random manner without regard to warp or a patterned in and out form.

VARIATIONS
- Wrap a single stick with yarns and fabrics for a woven stick.
- Find a grapevine wreath and weave and wrap materials through it.

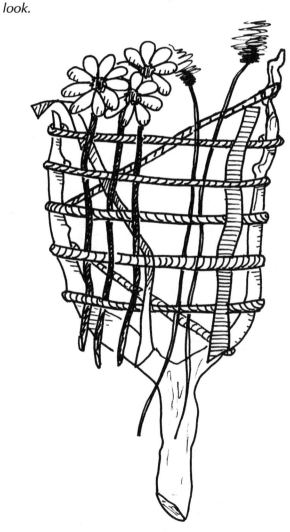

TRAY STITCHERY

The firmness of the grocery tray makes it easy for artists to hold and push the yarn through the styrofoam surface of the tray. Random stitching is a common first attempt, and when more experienced, artists plan patterns and scenes much like embroidery work. The creativity of tray stitchery is heavily dependent on the variety and colors of materials available.

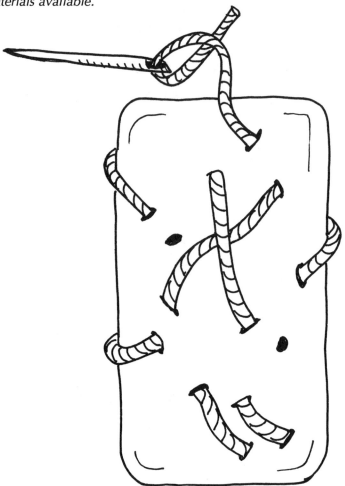

MATERIALS
clean styrofoam grocery tray
tool for poking holes such as –
   pencil
   scissors
   hole punch
   large plastic darning needle

yarn, colorful variety
tool for sewing such as –
   large plastic needle
   masking tape

PROCESS
1. Choose a process for poking holes in the tray:
   One is to pre-punch holes through the tray in any design or pattern with one of the poking tools such as a pencil. The other is to sew with a plastic darning needle, poking holes while sewing.
2. Tape the end of a piece of yarn with masking tape to form a needle, or a thread a plastic darning needle with yarn.
3. Push the taped end of the yarn through holes which were pre-punched. Sew in any fashion, in and out, around, through, here and there. Or, sew with the needle and yarn, punching holes while sewing.
4. Tape or tie the end of the yarn on the back of the tray when yarn runs out or when design is complete.
5. Continue with more yarn as desired.

HINTS
- Younger or less experienced artists do better with shorter pieces of yarn to prevent tangling. Once experienced, longer pieces of yarn work well.
- Leave space between two or more artists working in the same area so they don't poke each other when they pull the needle through the tray.

VARIATIONS
- Cover the styrofoam tray with starch and art tissue, dry, and then sew on the decorated tray.
- Sew on burlap, fabric, paper, or cardboard.
- Change colors or yarn, sew with thread, floss or fibers, string or fancy sewing trims like ribbon, bias tape, or lace.
- Cut slits in the edge of the tray and wrap the yarn instead of sewing. Experiment with weaving too.
- Cut slits in cardboard and wrap yarn through slits.
- Combine collage items in the stitching such as –
  pasta   buttons   cotton balls   beads   bits of fabric

SEWING BOARDS

MATERIALS
matte board or cardboard
paper
glue
hole punch, heavy duty
yarn
scissors
felt pens
tape

PROCESS
1. Prepare the matte board or cardboard by gluing a piece of colored paper to it if desired. Some cardboards come in colors so it may not be necessary. Also, brown cardboard has its own colorful character in browns and greys. Therefore, this step is optional.
2. Punch holes in the matte board or cardboard with a heavy duty hole punch. Some adult help may be needed if the cardboard is very thick. Punch the holes in any design or pattern desired.
3. Wrap the end of a piece of yarn with masking tape to make a "needle". Begin "sewing" the yarn in and out of the holes, across the cards, and in any direction. The yarn work may resemble weaving.
4. Change yarn by taping or tying the next piece of yarn to the first or to the back of the board.
5. When complete, tape or tie the last end to the back of the board.
6. Add colorful felt pen drawings or coloring between the yarn designs.

VARIATIONS
- Use other materials for sewing such as –
  sewing trim   ribbon   lace   thread
  embroidery floss   crochet thread   raffia   elastic
- Draw on the matte or cardboard first, and then string the yarn making a design along with the drawing.
- Glue a magazine picture or photograph to the card and then punch the holes and design with yarn.
- The card can be covered with clear contact paper, holes punched, and the sewing card for a small child will last longer.

Sometimes artists think making sewing boards is for the youngest artists only. There really is no age limit or creative limit to the possibilities of sewing on cardboard with varieties of colorful threads, yarns, and ribbons. Add felt pen design for an even more colorful experience.

DESIGN BOARD

 Hammering and nailing as art may be a new thought for some artists, but when the other art materials are added, the artistic experience is one of the more imaginative yet easy projects for all kids. Prepare for some loud pounding and imaginative approaches to sculpture.

MATERIALS
square of wood (8"x8" works well)
nails with heads
hammer
work table
materials for stringing on the nails, such as –

rubber bands	yarn	thread	string
sewing trims	floss	raffia	ribbon

collage items to add decoration, such as –

feathers	buttons	stickers	spools
straws	beads	pasta	cotton balls

PROCESS
1. Hammer nails into the wood square in any design. Be careful nails do not go all the way through into the table or floor. Short nails help solve the problem.
2. Weave, tie, stretch, and connect the nails with colored threads, yarn, rubber bands, or other materials.
3. Add or weave other collage items into the design board.
4. Materials can be removed and the board re-designed, or the original design can be saved or displayed.

VARIATIONS
- Cover the wood board with fabric, paint, or wallpaper before adding the nails.
- Nail a flip-top from an aluminum drink can on the back of the design board. Then hang the board like a picture or wall sculpture.
- Make a rubber band design which can be removed and used over and over again. Draw rubber band designs on pieces of paper, and then copy the designs on the board.
- Use a variety of wood shapes and sizes.
- Glue small pieces of wood scraps or picture frame pieces on the design board.
- Make a Nail Collage, p. 135.

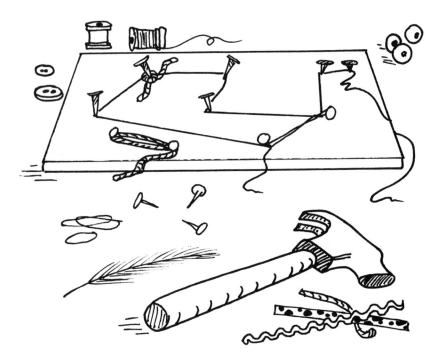

NAIL COLLAGE

MATERIALS
base wood piece, about 8"x8", or any other size
hammer
nails in all sizes and variety
work table

 A nail collage needs nothing more for creativity and art exploration than a piece of wood for the base, a hammer, and a bucket of nails of all types. Take advantage of the texture, height, and shine of the different nails to achieve design and visual form.

PROCESS
1. Hammer the nails into the wood square which is the base. The idea of this collage is to use the highs and lows of the nail heights to make a design. Also, the sizes of the nailheads will add to the design. Some nails are black and some are silvery, others are grey, and some are white. Use this for design and form. Nails can be very close together, or spaced farther apart. The design is completely up to the artist.
2. When the collage is complete, the nails can be pulled out again (some artists really enjoy this!), or the collage can be displayed.

VARIATIONS
*   Add other items into the collage such as those found in Design Board, p. 134. Add screws, nuts, bolts, and other hardware.
*   Cover the collage with aluminum foil, with nails poking through or with nails making a bumpy design under the foil.
*   Cover the board before beginning with foil, paint, paper, or fabric.

STRING THING

The artist wraps starched yarn or string around a balloon. When the string hardens and dries, the balloon is popped, and the stiffened string holds the shape of the balloon. String Things are fascinating and fun. Be sure they dry completely.

MATERIALS
about 30 pieces of colorful yarn or string, 3 feet long each
strong balloon
extra strong liquid starch (see ch. 7, p. 149)
bowl
newspaper
thread

PROCESS
1. Blow up the strong balloon and tie a double knot.
2. Place the balloon on the newspaper. Dip a piece of yarn in the extra strong starch. Soak it well, and then squeeze off the excess starch so the yarn isn't too heavy.
3. Begin wrapping the starched yarn around the balloon. Wrap in a crisscrossing fashion for a strong design.
4. Continue adding starched yarn until the balloon is well covered, but not too heavily covered or all the yarn will slide off.
5. Dry overnight.
6. Next day, pop the balloon and pull it out when completely dry.
7. Tie a thread to the top of the sculpture and hang it from the ceiling, a window header, or any other display area.

VARIATIONS
• A delicate string thing can be created with thread on a smaller balloon. Crochet thread and embroidery floss work well too.
• Colorful art tissue, glitter, and dyed white tissue or coffee filters can be added on top of the starched yarn for a globe design.
• Lightweight collage items can be tied or glued onto the completed string thing for further decoration.
• Papier-mâché is another art material that can be used in addition to the starch and yarn.

EASY PIÑATA

MATERIALS
inexpensive wallpaper paste (see p. 36 for homemade recipe)
newsprint or newspaper torn in strips and squares
large plastic bowl or tub
balloon
crepe paper
colored art tissue paper
collage materials

 One of the best uses for old newspaper is to soak it in wallpaper paste and cover just about anything, in this case a balloon. The paste and paper form a hard shell that when dry is perfect for making a festive piñata for even the youngest artists. It's true that papier-mâché is messy and engulfs an entire room in its ardor, but creating something from squishy newspaper that becomes so much more is worth the clean up.

PROCESS
1. Make wallpaper paste and pour into the plastic tub.
2. Tear newspaper into "biggish" strips and squares.
3. Blow up a balloon and tie with a double knot.
4. Place some newspaper strips into the wallpaper paste and cover them completely with paste.
5. Take out a strip and wrap it around the balloon, pressing down the edges and smoothing wrinkles.
6. Repeat the process until the balloon has about four layers covering it entirely. No balloon should show through.
7. Cover the balloon with one layer of crepe paper or colored tissue while the balloon is still wet with wallpaper paste. It is not necessary to dip the pieces in the tub of paste.
8. Dry completely for about three to four days.
9. When dry, paint the piñata with bright colors or leave as is.
10. Decorate the piñata with collage items or streamers to create animals, birds, fish, or abstract creations.
11. When dry again, cut a small opening in the top of the piñata, pop the balloon, and remove it. The piñata can be filled with treats, candy, surprises, or toys.

VARIATIONS
- Create a papier-mâché balloon purely for decoration and not as a piñata.
- Cover any form with papier-mâché such as a –

basket	cardboard tube
bottle	coconut shell
box	paper sculpture
box sculpture	plastic container
cardboard	wire sculpture

CONTACT TISSUE ART

 Sticking things without the mess or drying time of glue is an instantly pleasurable art experience. Clear contact paper becomes the bonding medium and colored art tissue the design medium. Add some scissors and some imaginative experimentation, and the project is ready to go.

MATERIALS
clear contact paper, about 8"x10" or a workable size
art tissue scraps and squares
scissors
small piece of yarn
hole punch

PROCESS
1. Cut a workable size of clear contact paper from the roll, perhaps about 8"x10" (although any size is fine).
2. Pull back half of the protective backing on the contact paper.
3. Press or fold it back, leaving the clear sticky half face up.
4. Cut or tear art tissue into shapes, designs, or pictures. Stick each one to the clear contact paper, pressing gently. Create a design, pattern, or a scene.
5. When complete, pull the remaining protective backing completely off.
6. Next, fold the clear side over the decorated side and press the two together with the hands.
7. Use scissors to trim edges or round corners. Snip or punch a little hole in the top of the design for a piece of yarn if the design will be hung in a window or other display area.

HINTS
• Contact paper can be unruly, so don't worry about perfection. Wrinkles, bubbles, and gaps are common, especially for younger or less experienced artists.

VARIATIONS
• Combine other art materials in the contact paper work such as dry weeds and flowers, doilies, lace, crayon shavings, glitter, feathers, yarn, sand, or confetti.
• Design holiday ornaments.
• Design ideas for a mobile.

TISSUE GLASS

MATERIALS
liquid starch or thinned white glue in a cup
paintbrush
colored art tissue scraps and squares
glass jar or vase
newspaper
clear hobby paint (optional)

 Colored art tissue comes in a rainbow of colors. The scraps from other art experiences can be starched or glued to glass to create a translucent vase, bank, or pencil jar. The tissue covering helps prevent the glass from breaking. Place the finished project in a sunny window to enjoy the look of stained glass.

PROCESS
1. Place the jar right side up on a piece of newspaper.
2. With liquid starch or a mixture of white glue and water, brush an area of the jar to begin.
3. Stick a torn piece of art tissue, or a cut square of art tissue on the sticky area. Brush over the piece with more starch or glue.
4. Add more pieces of tissue, overlapping the edges, and sticking down all the edges. Stick tissue pieces over the edge of the mouth of the jar too.
5. Turn the jar over and finish by covering the base of the jar.
6. Dry overnight.
7. When dry, an adult can coat the jar or vase with a glaze of clear hobby paint for shine and protection. Dry.

VARIATIONS
• Make the jar into a bank. Cut a slot in the jar lid by hammering a chisel point into the lid. Then hammer the other side of the lid to flatten the raw edges of the slot.
• Add other types of paper, bits of doilies, confetti, or pieces of flowers and weeds into the covering of the jar.
• Use tissue on wood scraps, bottles, rocks, a piece of glass in a picture frame, waxed paper, paper, clear plastic wrap or styrofoam grocery trays.

FABRIC STENCIL

 Stenciling on fabric is made easy by using shapes cut from contact paper. Using fabric dye, crayons, pens or chalk, draw around or over the stencil. When the contact stencil is removed, you have a permanent fabric design that will wash and dry and keep its bright color for years.

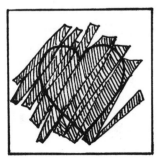

stencil on

stencil removed

MATERIALS

contact paper (patterned or clear)
scissors
fabric to stencil, such as –

plain muslin	pillow case	wall hanging
sheet	pillow	quilt squares
T-shirt	apron	baby duvet

any fabric coloring medium such as –

| fabric pens | fabric dye and brushes |
| fabric chalk | fabric crayons |

(follow the directions on the box of any of the above)

PROCESS

1. Choose a fabric coloring medium such as fabric pens.
2. Cut out a shape from contact paper. Remove the protective backing.
3. Stick the shape on fabric, pressing the edges down.
4. Cut as many shapes as needed to decorate the fabric. Stick them on the fabric.
5. Using fabric pens or other coloring medium, draw and color over the stick-on shapes and onto the fabric. Stenciling around the shapes works too. Follow any further directions on the fabric color box.
6. Remove the shapes and reveal a clean, crisp design where the shape used to be.
7. For laundering fabric, follow directions on the box. Most fabrics can be washed and dried without loosing the color from the pens or paints.

VARIATIONS

- A negative stencil is made by drawing inside the stencil and a positive stencil by drawing around the stencil.
- Follow the contact paper stencil idea on paper. Or cut paper shapes and rubber cement them to paper. Then paint or color over and around them. Remove the stencils when a design is complete.
- Spatter fabric paint on the fabric with a toothbrush rubbed across a piece of window screen as described on p. 78. Use contact paper for the stencils instead of leaves or paper.

FESTIVE BANNER

MATERIALS
bright fabric in a long, narrow shape
iron
two sticks or dowels, a bit longer than the width of the fabric
sewing machine for adult
yarn threaded on large plastic needle, optional
tempera paints in cups
paintbrushes
newspaper
string (a little longer than one stick)

PROCESS
1. To prepare the fabric for the banner, an adult can iron the banner fabric to remove wrinkles. An adult can then sew a casing or tube at the top and the bottom of the banner wide enough to fit the dowels tightly.
2. Insert the dowels into the casings. Fit should be tight but dowel should slide easily.
3. For optional decoration, the artist can stitch with the needle and yarn through the fabric, next to the casing, in any stitch or design. Knot the yarn on the back of the banner to hold.
4. Using tempera paints, paint designs, patterns, or pictures on the banner. It may be necessary to tape the banner to the table to control slipping.
5. Dry completely.
6. Tie string each at end of the dowel in the top of the banner where it pokes out of the casing. Hang the banner from this string on a hook in the wall or other hanging area.

HINT
- Tempera paints can soak through the fabric, so be sure to work on a table covered with newspaper or butcher paper.
- Tempera paint can smudge or stain clothing when a banner is carried so be careful.

VARIATIONS
- Create a banner to celebrate a special day, a season, or a holiday.
- Use other fabric coloring mediums to decorate the banner such as fabric pens, paints, chalk or crayons.
- Experiment with stencils, potato prints, fabric transfers, and other ideas on fabric.
- Make an assortment of banners to change monthly or seasonally to celebrate the seasons or holidays through banner display.

What better way is there to decorate and brighten a room than with a fabric banner painted with festive tempera paint? The banner can be changed at any time by removing the dowels and then reinserting them in a different banner. Keep a supply of banners ready to decorate and celebrate special days, holidays, or the seasons.

PRESSED FLOWERS

 Pressed flowers and weeds are delicate and lovely and lend themselves to infinite creative arrangements. Glue them in designs on paper like painting a beautiful picture.

MATERIALS
fresh flowers and blossoming weeds
ferns, grasses, and leaves
newspaper
heavy books
glue in a dish
tweezers
toothpicks
heavy paper

PROCESS
1. Go for a walk and collect fresh flowers or blossoming weeds, including buttercups, chamomile, and daisies, leaves, ferns, and lacy grasses.
2. Spread them out on newspaper with space between each one. The flowers and weeds should not touch.
3. Place several more sheets of newspaper on top of the flowers. Then place books on top of the paper to press. Use any flat, heavy weight on top of the flowers such as a carpet or heavy boxes.
4. Wait for about four weeks for the flowers to thoroughly dry out, keeping in mind that the thicker flowers take the longest.
5. Remove the heavy books, peel back the newspaper, and carefully handle the delicate dried, pressed flowers.
6. Dip a toothpick in the white glue and touch it to the paper. Then pick up the dried flower with fingers or with tweezers and place it on the glued area. Add other dried blossoms and flowers to make an arrangement on the paper. Dry completely.

VARIATIONS
- Make bookmarks, note cards, or framed flower designs.
- Cover flower creations with clear contact paper or plastic wrap.
- Arrange flowers under glass in a picture frame.
- Glue flowers on a paper circle which can then be glued to a wooden curtain rod ring as a frame. The hook on the ring becomes the hanger for a wall decoration.
- Glue pressed flowers to fabric, grocery tray, block of wood, driftwood, or a rock.

NATURE PRESSING

MATERIALS
delicate flowers, weeds, and grasses
2 pieces of Plexiglas or heavy acetate the same size
wide, cloth library tape
colored art tissue, optional
scissors
paper clip

 When a single flower begins to fade but is too beautiful to throw away, it can be pressed between two sheets of Plexiglas for a permanent nature pressing to enjoy for years to come.

PROCESS
1. Buy two pieces of Plexiglas or heavy acetate the same size.
2. Find a flower or weed to frame and display.
3. Place the flower on one sheet of Plexiglas. Add other little leaves, grasses, ferns, or bits of colored art tissue.
4. Place the other piece of Plexiglas over the nature display.
5. Slip a paper clip between the pieces of plastic to form a hanger.
5. With adult help, take wide library cloth tape and go around the edges of the doubled plastic forming a tape frame that also holds the two sheets together.
6. Hang on the wall or from a string in a sunny window.

VARIATIONS
- Press a flower or weed between two pieces of glass and epoxy glue the edges. Adult supervision.
- Press a piece of nature between two sheets of contact paper, iron between wax papers, starch between clear plastic wrap, or place under the glass of a picture frame.

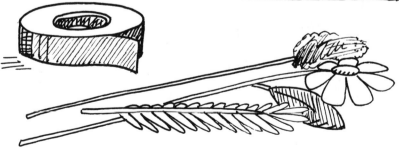

WREATH OF NATURE

Collecting things from nature all year round and saving them for making a wreath adds to the creativity and imagination of wreath making. Use lots of glue and a good sturdy base so the wreath can be filled to overflowing with the bounties of nature.

MATERIALS
extra heavy cardboard, 2 pieces
glue, scissors, pencil
large and small bowls for tracing circles
loop of wire or heavy cord, about 6 inches long
nature materials, such as –
      pine cones, nuts, dried leaves, dried grasses,
      seed pods, thistles, corn or corn cobs, etc.
raffia, ribbon, or sewing trims
glue gun, optional (with adult supervision)
clear gloss craft paint (optional)

PROCESS
1. Trace around a large bowl on both cardboard pieces. Then place a small bowl in the center of the first large circles and trace.
2. Cut the two wreath shapes with scissors. Adult help will be needed for this tough job.
3. Glue both pieces of cardboard wreath together to make a strong form for the wreath. The use of a glue gun can expedite the drying and hold of glue, but must be supervised by an adult.
4. Punch two small holes in the top of the cardboard wreath and insert a loop of wire or heavy cord.
5. Glue pine cones, nuts, dried leaves, corncobs, and other nature materials to the cardboard. Use lots of glue and fill the wreath covering the cardboard rings beneath. Again, a glue gun can be used but must be completely supervised by an adult.
6. Wrap, tie, or glue raffia or other decoration to the wreath.
7. Dry overnight or longer on a flat table or shelf. Do not hang until dry.
8. When dry, an adult can spray the wreath with a clear hobby paint for a glossy effect.
9. Hang to enjoy, or use as a centerpiece.

VARIATIONS
- Use as a table centerpiece and place a candle in a glass jar in the center.
- Add non-natural materials such as Christmas decorations, tinsel, glitter, confetti, or gold and silver sprayed pine cones and pasta.
- Make a wreath from "junk" or a wreath with a theme, such as –

hair rollers	litter	hardware
toy parts	family photos	food

LANTERNS

MATERIALS

water	hammer	mittens
coffee can	nails	towel
freezer	punch can-opener	candle, matches

Artists who enjoy using their muscles, using hammer and nails, and working through a process that feels like building and fixing will particularly enjoy creating lanterns from coffee cans.

PROCESS
1. Fill the coffee can with water and freeze until hard, at least overnight.
2. Place a towel on the floor and set the frozen can on the towel.
3. Put on mittens. Take a hammer and nail and makes holes in the can in any pattern or design. The ice will keep the can from collapsing and bending.
4. With a punch can-opener, make several holes in the side edge of the bottom rim of the can to draw air for the candle.
5. When satisfied with the design, let the ice thaw. Drain the can and dry completely. Be very careful of sharp edges.
6. With adult supervision, place a fat candle inside the lantern and carefully light with a match. Use outdoors or indoors.

VARIATIONS
* Use other cans, especially the large sizes, such as –
  soup   vegetables   tomato sauce   juice
* Decorate the can with permanent felt pens.
* A nail hammered through the center of the bottom of the can, from the outside in, makes a secure candle holder. Press the candle carefully onto the nail.
* Holes can be punched in the top rim of the can and then wires attached for a hanging lantern.
* Themes or designs can be punctured into the can for holiday or party lanterns such as a Christmas tree shape, a star, or a firework explosion shape.
* Names and messages can be hammered in the can.

PUPPET TREASURE BOX

Puppets open a world of pretend, self-expression, and communication. Fill a box with any of the five completed puppet creations listed. Provide materials for artists to think up their own puppet creations because even a can of soup can be a hilarious expressive puppet to a child. The five puppets ideas are: Stick, Walking, Sock, Spoon, and Free.

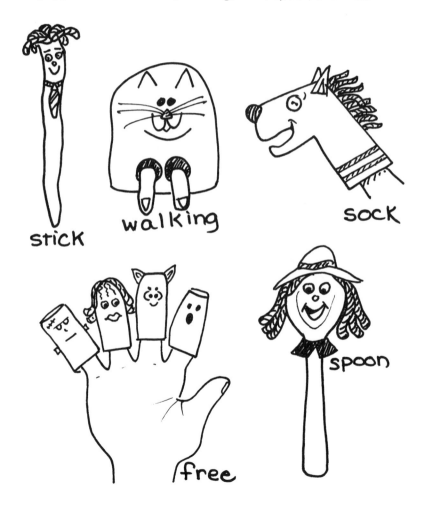

stick
walking
sock
free
spoon

MATERIALS for each puppet idea

1. STICK PUPPET
cardboard
colored paper
stick

2. WALKING PUPPET
heavy paper
crayons

3. SOCK PUPPET
sock
sewing trims
fabric glue
needle, thread

4. SPOON PUPPET
wooden spoon
fabric scraps
yarn, wool

5. FREE PUPPET
fabric
felt
craft sticks
collage materials

ALL PUPPETS
may need –
scissors
glue
tape
felt pens

PROCESS

1. Choose a type of puppet to create. See illustrations for the basic idea of what each puppet can be like. Use your own ideas based on these, or think up new ones.
2. Glue, paint or decorate puppet bases, such as –
STICK PUPPET – Draw and cut out double paper shapes to glue on the stick. Glue one on the front, and one on the back for a strong puppet. Or, decorate the stick with felt pens to be a very skinny puppet.
WALKING PUPPET – Draw with crayon or felt pen on heavy paper. Or glue a drawing to heavy paper. Cut out the drawing and then add two holes cut near the bottom of the drawing for two fingers to poke through. The fingers become the puppet's legs or means of motion.
SOCK PUPPET – Decorate an old sock with felt, ribbon, yarn, buttons, and other materials. Use clear craft glue, white glue, or sew with a needle and thread. Glue with the sock on the non-drawing hand to prevent sticking the sock together and to see how the puppet is progressing in character. Craft eyes are good too.
SPOON PUPPET – Paint the wooden spoon or leave it natural. Decorate the spoon by gluing yarn, collage materials, craft eyes, and so on. Features can be glued, painted, or drawn with felt pens. Clothing can be added with fabric scraps, foil, wallpaper, or paper.
FREE PUPPET – Use mittens, gloves, felt sewn tubes to fit oven fingers, tin cans, milk cartons, or a stale bagel for the beginnings of a free puppet. Anything can be a puppet. Have fun and enjoy the show!

VARIATIONS

- Make up puppet shows, if desired.
- Decorate a cardboard box to store puppets.

RESOURCE GUIDE
chapter 7

Quick Recipe-Formula Guide

Baker's Clay –

There are many recipes similar to this one, but this is one that is versatile, soft, pliable and either bakes or air dries nicely. Mix 4 cups flour, 1 cup salt, and 1-3/4 cups warm water in a bowl. (If a colored dough is desired, add food coloring or tempera paint to the water first.) Knead for 5-10 minutes. Model objects and sculptures. Bake at 300°F for 1-3 hours, or air dry for a few days. Glaze with egg white, evaporated milk, or mayonnaise before baking. Or paint with a clear varnish or fixative after baking and cooling. This recipe can be halved, doubled, or tripled, but measure carefully.

Bread Clay –

Mix 2/3 cup warm water and 1/2 cup salt in a bowl. Add 2 cups flour and stir. Knead. Model and explore dough. Bake objects at 225°-250°F for 4 to 6 hours. Objects should be hard on both sides.

Bubble Print –

Mix a solution of equal parts water and liquid dish detergent. Let stand overnight.

Chalk and Sugar Water –

Mix 1/2 cup water and 2 tablespoons sugar. Stir until dissolved. Dip chalk into sugar-water and then draw or color. Drawings are bright and less smudgy, but they still smudge some.

Cornstarch and Baking Soda Dough –

Mix 1 cup cornstarch, 2 cups baking soda, and 1-1/4 cup water in a pan over medium heat, stirring constantly until thick like dough. Food coloring may be worked in when cooled slightly on a breadboard or piece of foil. Keep covered. Roll, cut, model in small shapes.

Cornstarch and Salt Dough –

Mix 1 cup salt, 1 cup cornstarch, and 1/2 cup boiling water (and food coloring or tempera paint). Mix over low heat, stirring until mixture is too stiff to stir. When cool, knead until smooth. Model. Dry. Paint.

Cornstarch Beads –

Mix all of the following in a bowl: 3/4 cup flour, 1/2 cup cornstarch, 1/2 cup salt, food coloring or powdered tempera if desired. Then add 3/8 cup warm water gradually. Knead, adding a dusting of flour to help prevent dough from sticking to the hands. Pinch pieces for beads, roll into balls, and pierce each bead with a plastic darning needle or toothpick. Dry for a few days. Sometimes holes need to be re-pierced. Dough stays colorful when dry. Beads may be coated with a clear enamel when dry.

Cornstarch Mixture –

Use as an alternative to wallpaper paste. Add 2 tablespoons of cornstarch to cold water, enough to form a paste. Add 1 cup cold water and then cook on the stove until it reaches a thickness like custard. Add a little warm water to thin if necessary. Store in the fridge.

Vegetable Dye Paint (see food coloring) –

Dissolve 1/8 teaspoon vegetable food dye in powder form in a tablespoon of water. Add it to wallpaper paste, to a mixture of cornstarch and water (recipe above), or to liquid starch. The paint is translucent and brilliant. It will not cover lettering on boxes or newspapers like tempera paint.

Fingerpaint: 2 easy recipes that work –

1. Mix liquid starch and powdered or liquid tempera paint on the paper and mix by hand. Then fingerpaint.

2. Boil 3 parts water and remove from heat. Dissolve 1 part cornstarch in a little cold water, and then add to the hot water stirring constantly. Boil until clear and thick. Add powdered tempera paint. Use while still warm or cool.

Fingerpainting with Whipped Soap Flakes –

Put 2 cups warm water in a bowl. Start mixer, and then add 1 cup soap flakes. Beat until stiff. Use as a white fingerpaint, or add tempera or food coloring mixing thoroughly. Use as a fingerpaint. Do not wash this paint down the drain as it will clog the pipes. This mixture can also: be used in a cake decorating tube, glittered without glue, and will dry like frosting. Warning: Looks good enough to eat but definitely isn't!

Foil or Plastic Painting (cottage cheese containers, yogurt, frozen dinner trays) –

Mix 1/2 cup of tempera paint powder with 1 teaspoon liquid dishwashing detergent for a thick paint. Test the paint on foil or plastic. If it does not stick, add about 1/2 teaspoon more of dishwashing liquid.

Food Coloring –

Widely available in little liquid squeeze bottles in the grocery store. Also comes in paste form which is more color intense, from cake decorating departments and hobby stores. Best of all, powdered vegetable food dye called Edicol is available in bulk which will last for many years for a preschool or a lifetime for a family. Edicol colors can be mixed together to create new colors. To make the paint or dye, mix Edicol with about 1 T. water and then add 1/8 teaspoon of dye and stir. Add more dye for brilliant colors, or less for paler colors. Available at educational shops. OR use food coloring as a substitute.

Glue, Thinned –

Squeeze some white glue (Elmer's Glue or Elmer's School Glue is a common brand) into a jar or dish and mix in water with a paint brush until the glue is thin and "paints" easily with a brush on paper. Tempera paint or food coloring can be added to thinned glue to make a colored glue.

Goop –

Mix one part cornstarch with one part water in a pan. Use hands, spoons, and cups to explore Goop.

Pasta, Colored –

Mix food coloring with cold water. (If using Edicol, mix about 1/8 teaspoon with a medium size bowl full of water.) Place dry pasta into the dye, swirl it around, and then remove the pasta, placing it on a thick pad of newspaper to dry. Move the pasta about while drying so it won't stick to the paper. You may wish to wear rubber gloves during this entire process.

Playdough (my favorite) –

Mix and cook on low in a pan until a ball forms: 1 cup flour, 1 cup water, 1 cup salt, 1 tablespoon cream of tartar. Leave natural or color with food coloring, tempera, Kook-aid, Jello, or watercolor paint. Knead and then use warm or cool. Store in airtight container.

Pressed Flowers and Leaves –

Collect fresh flowers and leaves and lay them out on newspaper so they aren't touching. Place several more sheets of newspaper on top of them. Then put books, a carpet, or anything flat and heavy on top of the newspaper. Leave for about four weeks to dry completely. Thick items will take longer. Use for note cards, book marks, or other pressed flower arrangements.

Puffy Paint Dough –

Mix equal parts of flour and salt and water to form a paste. Separate dough into bowls and add powdered tempera paint to each one. Then place the colored dough into squeeze bottles. Squeeze onto heavy paper like frosting. Do not eat.

Salt and Flour Beads –

Mix 1 cup salt, 1 cup flour, 1 T. alum. Add and mix water to a consistency of putty (add tempera paint or food coloring if desired). Pinch off dough and shape into beads. Pierce bead with plastic needle or toothpick. Dry.

Salt Modeling –

Mix 1 part salt with 1 part flour in a bowl. Add enough water to make a thick frosting-like dough (about 2/3 part water). Stir. Color can be added now with food coloring or paint. Spread mixture on cardboard for maps or dioramas, making hills and valleys. Dry for 1-2 days. Paint and/or decorate when dry.

Sawdust Modeling –

1. Mix 4 cups sawdust, 1 cup wheat paste, and 2-1/2 cups water together. Paint or color is optional. Model. Dry.

2. Mix 2 cups sawdust and 1 cup flour. Then add water until dough is squishy and stiff. Knead. Model. Sand and paint, optional.

Scribble Cookies –

Save stub ends of old crayons, peel, and break into pieces. Sort into muffin tins either by individual colors, or by a mixture of rainbow colors. Place muffin tin in a warm oven turned off for about 10 minutes. Watch at all times. Crayons should melt and soften, float in a liquid, but not melt completely to total liquid. Remove and cool. Or freeze for easiest removal of scribble cookies. Use to color, for rubbings, and other crayon uses.

Starch, Homemade Liquid –

Dissolve 1 teaspoon granulated starch in a little bit of water. Stir and add 1 cup of hot water. Bring this to a boil for about 1 minute, stirring constantly. When cool, store in a container with an airtight lid. Lasts a long time.

Starch, Homemade Liquid and Extra Strong –

Substitute 1 tablespoon of granulated starch for 1 teaspoon and follow the directions for Homemade Liquid Starch above.

Wallpaper Paste –

Use the type made for lightweight wallpapers and crafts. Follow the directions on the box, but use cold water and don't worry about any lumps. They will dissolve after a few hours. Paste keeps a few days if kept in a container with a tight lid. After that, the smell will tell! Or make your own with the following recipe.

Wallpaper Paste, Homemade –

Mix 4 cups flour and 1 cup sugar in a large pan. Add enough water to make a smooth paste, about 1 gallon. Boil on the stove, stirring until thick and clear. Then thin with 1 quart cold water. Add oil of cinnamon to keep paste fresh smelling. Use with papier-mâché projects.

COLLAGE MATERIALS LIST

The following list of collage and construction materials are suggestions to help you make a collection of materials for use in collage and other art projects. Of course you do not have to keep all of these items on hand. Collect them and accumulate them at your convenience. You may want to select items to help teach certain concepts or save a particular type of item (for example, all natural items). Suitable containers are such items as:

> plastic bags, plastic storage containers, oatmeal boxes, shoe boxes, soup cans, coffee cans, and more.

A
acorns
allspice
almonds
aluminum foil
apple seeds
apricot seeds

B
ball bearing
balsa wood
bamboo
bark
basket reeds
beads
beans
belts
bias tape
blotter paper
bobby pins
bolts and nuts
bones
bottle caps
bottles
boxes
brads
braiding
broken parts
broken toys
buckles
burlap scraps

C
cancelled stamps
candles
candy wrappers
cardboard scraps
carpet samples
carpet warp
cellophane scraps
cellophane tape
chains
chalk
checkers
clock parts
clothespins
cloth scraps
cloves
coffee filters
coffee grounds
coins
comb
confetti
construction paper scraps
contact paper
cord
corks
corn husks
corn kernels
costume jewelry
cotton
cotton balls
crepe paper scraps
crystals

D
dice
dominoes
drapery samples
dried beans and peas
dried flowers
dried grass
dried seeds
driftwood
dry cereals

E
Easter grass
egg cartons
eggshells
elastic
emery boards
embroidery floss
erasers
evergreens
eyelets
excelsior

F
fabric
faucet washers
feathers
felt scraps
film cartridges
film spools
filters
fish tank gravel
fishing lures
flashbulbs
flocking
florist's foil, foam, tape
flowers
flowers, artificial
flowers, dried
flowers, plastic
form packing
fur samples

G
gauze
gift wrap
glass beads
glass mosaic pieces
glitter
gold thread
gold jewelry parts
grains
gravel
gummed labels
gummed paper reinforcements
gummed paper

H
hair netting
hairpins
hair roller
hardware scraps
hat trimmings
hooks

I
ice cream sticks
inner tube scraps

J
jewelry pieces
jewelry wire
junk of all kinds
jute

K
key rings
key tabs
keys

L
lace
laminated items
leather scraps
leaves
lentils
lids
linoleum scraps

M
macaroni
mailing tubes
map pins
marbles
masonite
meat trays, paper
meat trays, plastic
meat trays, styrofoam
metal scraps
metal shavings
mirrors
mosquito netting
moss, dried

N
nails
newspaper
noodles, dry
noodles, wet
nut cups
nuts

O
oilcloth scraps
orange seeds
orange sticks
origami paper
ornaments

P
paint chips
paper baking cups
paper clips
paper dots
paper fasteners
paper products, all kinds
paper tubes
pebbles
pill bottles
pillboxes
pine cones
pine needles
ping-pong balls
pins, all kinds
pipe cleaners
pits

plastic, all kinds
plastic bottles
plastic foam
plastic scraps
popcorn
potatoes
pumpkin seeds

Q
Q-tips
quartz crystals
quills

R
raffia
recording tape
rhinestones
ribbon
rice
rickrack
rock salt
rocks
rope pieces
rubber bands
rubber tubing

S
safety pins
salt crystals
sandpaper
sawdust
scouring pads
screening, plastic or wire
screws
seals, gummed
seam binding
seashells
seedpods
seeds
sequins
sewing tape
shoe laces
shot
silk scraps
skewers, bamboo
skewers, wooden
soap
soldering wire
spaghetti
sponges
spools
spray can lids
stamps, all kinds
stars, bummer
steel wool
sticks

stones
straws, broom
straws, drinking
straws, stirring
string
styrofoam

T
tape, cellophane
tape, library
tape, masking
tape, mystic
tape, plastic
tape, Scotch
tape, sewing
telephone wire
thistles
thread
tiles
tinker toy parts
tissue paper
tongue depressors
toothbrushes
toothpicks
torn paper scraps
twigs
twine

V
velvet scraps
vermiculite

W
wallpaper
warp
washers
wax candles
weeds
wood scraps
wood shavings
wooden beads
wooden dowels
wooden wheels
wool
wrapping papers

X
X-rays

Y
yarns

Z
zippers

INDEXES

MATERIALS INDEX

Portraits of Aunt MaryAnn

Brittany Kohl, 9

Rachel Kohl, 7

Andrew Kohl, 4

Brittany, Rachel, and Andrew Kohl, MaryAnn's nieces and nephew, are the children of Steven and Louise Kohl, Bremerton, Washington. The Kohl kids are home-schooled and enjoy art experiences from Aunt MaryAnn's books.

As a child growing up in Longmeadow, Massachusetts MaryAnn Kohl enjoyed art, music, reading, and playing outside. Her most treasured possessions were a box of pastel chalks, her Indian Princess bicycle with three gears and a generator for the lights on the front and back, and a Ginny doll with lots of clothes.

Later on MaryAnn added working on the yearbook staff and cheerleading to her interests. She continued to ride her bike, draw, and play with her Ginny doll! Dating also took on a new importance as did driving her first car.

MaryAnn later received a BS in Education from Old Dominion University, Norfolk, VA, and a graduate degree from Western Washington University, Bellingham, WA in Elementary Education, English, Speech, and Drama. Her favorite college classes were Music Education, Art Education, and Greek Mythology.

After teaching elementary education for ten years, MaryAnn retired to raise her family. She gradually began to write art books for children while teaching art workshops, and eventually started her own publishing company, Bright Ring Publishing.

She still loves to draw, read, and ride her bike when she finds the time, and to drive her favorite car. She lives with her husband and two daughters in Bellingham, Washington.

ORDER FORM

Bright Ring Publishing

P.O. Box 5768 • Bellingham, WA 98227
(206) 734-1601 / FAX (206) 676-1271
800-480-4ART for orders

Name_____

Address_____

City_____ State_____ Zip_____

Phone: (_____)_____

Qty.	Title of Book	Price Each	Price
	SCRIBBLE ART *Independent Creative Art for Children*	$14.95	
	MUDWORKS *Creative Clay, Dough and Modeling*	$14.95	
	GOOD EARTH ART *Environmental Art for Kids*	$16.95	
	SCIENCE ARTS *Discovering Science Through Art Experiences*	$15.95	
	PRESCHOOL ART *It's the Process Not the Product*	$19.95	

Total for books	
Deduct 10% for orders of 4 or more books	
SUBTOTAL	
Sales Tax @ 7.8% (Washington only)	
Shipping (see chart)	
TOTAL ENCLOSED	

Please make checks payable to:
Bright Ring Publishing.

SHIPPING CHART

USPS Book Rate, 4th Class:
$2.50 – 1st Book $1.00 – each additional

UPS and AirMail:
$4.00 – 1st book $2.00 – each additional

Orders shipped within 3 business days.
Allow 2 weeks for shipment to arrive.

BRIGHT IDEAS BOOKSHELF

Bright Ring Publishing encourages the creative ability of each child by producing quality art idea books that inspire exploration and discovery through art process. We like to say, "Process not Product!" because the process of creating and exploring art is more important than the final product. All of the books in our Bright Ideas for Learning series build upon the natural curiosity and creativity of children of all ages. Everyone can be an artist.

MAK

MaryAnn Kohl
publisher and author

ALL NEW

SCRIBBLE ART
Independent Creative Art Experiences for Children
(originally published as SCRIBBLE COOKIES)

11x8-1/2 • 160 pages • $14.95 • paperback
ISBN 0-935607-05-6

Over 200 process art ideas that stress exploration in an independent, non-competitive, open-ended setting. Activities need only basic art supplies and common kitchen materials. Three Indexes, charted Table of Contents, child-tested activities. Ideal for any age, for home, school, or child care.

❖ 1991 Daycare Directors Choice Award ❖

MUDWORKS
Creative Clay, Dough, and Modeling Experiences

11x8-1/2 • 152 pages • $14.95 • paperback
ISBN 0-935607-02-1

Anyone who likes to play in mud, playdough, papier-mache and similar mediums will love this book of over 125 clays, doughs, and modeling mixtures. Uses common household materials and requires no expertise. Ideal for fun or serious art for all ages, for home, school, or child care.

❖ 1991 Benjamin Franklin Award ❖
❖ 1990 American Library Assn. Starred Review ❖

SCIENCE ARTS
Discovering Science Through Art Experiences

11x8-1/2 • 144 pages • $15.95 • paperback
ISBN 0-935607-04-8

Children 3-10 learn basic science concepts as they explore over 200 amazing and beautiful art experiences using common household materials. Projects are open-ended and easy to do. One science-art experiment per page, fully illustrated. Includes three indexes and a charted Table of Contents. Suitable for home, school, or child care.

❖ 1994 Benjamin Franklin Award ❖
❖ 1994 National Press Communicator Award ❖

GOOD EARTH ART
Environmental Art For Kids

11x8-1/2 • 224 pages • $16.95 • paperback
ISBN 0-935607-01-3

Over 200 art projects that develop an awareness of the environment and a caring attitude towards the earth. Uses common materials collected from nature or recycled from trash. Filled with simple ideas to recycle and create for all ages. Includes charted Table of Contents, two indexes, and a list of environmental resources.

❖ 1992 Benjamin Franklin Award ❖

PRESCHOOL ART
It's the Process Not the Product

11x8-1/2 • 260 pages • $19.95 • paperback
ISBN 0-87659-168-3

Over 250 process-oriented art experiences designed for children 3-6, but ideal for all ages. Uses materials commonly found in the home or school. Organized by months and seasons. Index. Published by Gryphon House, Inc., Beltsville, MD.